THE
BEST LOVED HOME BALLADS

of

James Whitcomb Riley

Fredonia Books
Amsterdam, The Netherlands

The Best Loved Home Ballads of James Whitcomb Riley

by
James Whitcomb Riley

ISBN: 1-58963-357-1

Copyright © 2001 by Fredonia Books

Reprinted from the 1931 edition

Fredonia Books
Amsterdam, The Netherlands
http://www.fredoniabooks.com

All rights reserved, including the right to reproduce this book, or portions thereof, in any form.

In order to make original editions of historical works available to scholars at an economical price, this facsimile of the original edition of 1931 is reproduced from the best available copy and has been digitally enhanced to improve legibility, but the text remains unaltered to retain historical authenticity.

THE BEST LOVED HOME BALLADS
OF JAMES WHITCOMB RILEY

CONTENTS

	PAGE
At "The Literary"	35
August	62
Back from Town	64
Barefoot Boy, A	17
Boys, The	69
Canary at the Farm, A	215
Cassander	187
Child's Home—Long Ago, A	197
Country Pathway, A	18
Cuored o' Skeerin'	164
Decoration Day on the Place	73
Doc Sifers	154
Down around the River	159
Down to the Capital	39
Dream of Autumn, A	66
Farmer Whipple.—Bachelor	166
Fessler's Bees	87
Few of the Bird-Family, A	24
First Bluebird, The	70
Full Harvest, A	25
Griggsby's Station	107
Herr Weiser	48
His Pa's Romance	119

	PAGE
His Room	161
"Home Ag'in"	179
Home at Night	214
Home-Folks	201
Hoosier Folk-Child, The	203
Hoosier Spring-Poetry	217
Hoss, The	101
Knee-Deep in June	110
"Last Christmas Was a Year Ago"	79
Marthy Ellen	50
'Mongst the Hills o' Somerset	174
Mulberry Tree, The	223
Old Band, The	76
Old-Fashioned Roses	105
Old Home by the Mill, The	29
Old John Henry	177
Old Man and Jim, The	44
Old Man's Memory, An	53
Old Man's Nursery Rhyme	221
Old October	13
Old Trundle-Bed, The	97
Old Winters on the Farm	28
On the Banks o' Deer Crick	219
Poems Here at Home, The	11
Rabbit	115
Rambo-Tree, The	134
Right Here at Home	26
Somep'n Common-Like	31

CONTENTS—CONCLUDED

	PAGE
Summer's Day, A	139
Symptoms	117
Tale of the Airly Days, A	142
Thoughts fer the Discuraged Farmer	136
Town and Country	71
Tree-Toad, The	15
Uncle Dan'l in Town over Sunday	149
Up and Down Old Brandywine	144
Us Farmers in the Country	195
Voice from the Farm, A	200
We Must Get Home	191
What Smith Knew about Farming	207
When the Frost Is on the Punkin	59
When the Green Gits Back in the Trees	152
Where the Children Used to Play	99
Wortermelon Time	55
Writin' Back to the Home-Folks	32

THE BEST LOVED HOME BALLADS
OF JAMES WHITCOMB RILEY

THE POEMS HERE AT HOME

THE Poems here at Home!—Who'll write 'em
   down,
   Jes' as they air—in Country and in Town?
Sowed thick as clods is 'crost the fields and lanes,
Er these-'ere little hop-toads when it rains!—
Who'll "voice" 'em? as I heerd a feller say
'At speechified on Freedom, t'other day,
And soared the Eagle tel, it 'peared to me,
She wasn't bigger'n a bumble-bee!

Who'll sort 'em out and set 'em down, says I,
'At's got a stiddy hand enough to try
To do 'em jestice 'thout a-foolin' some,
And headin' facts off when they want to come?—
Who's got the lovin' eye, and heart, and brain
To reco'nize 'at nothin's made in vain—
'At the Good Bein' made the bees and birds
And brutes first choice, and us-folks afterwards?

What We want, as I sense it, in the line
O' poetry is somepin' Yours and Mine—
Somepin' with live stock in it, and out-doors,
And old crick-bottoms, snags, and sycamores:
Putt weeds in—pizen-vines, and underbresh,
As well as johnny-jump-ups, all so fresh
And sassy-like!—and groun'-squir'ls,—yes, and "We,"
As sayin' is,—"We, Us and Company!"

Putt in old Nature's sermonts,—them's the best,—
And 'casion'ly hang up a hornets' nest
'At boys 'at's run away from school can git
At handy-like—and let 'em tackle it!
Let us be wrought on, of a truth, to feel
Our proneness fer to hurt more than we heal,
In ministratin' to our vain delights—
Fergittin' even insec's has their rights!

No "Ladies' Amaranth," ner "Treasury" book—
Ner "Night Thoughts," nuther—ner no "Lally Rook"!
We want some poetry 'at's to Our taste,
Made out o' truck 'at's jes' a-goin' to waste
'Cause smart folks thinks it's altogether too
Outrageous common—'cept fer me and you!—
Which goes to argy, all sich poetry
Is 'bliged to rest its hopes on You and Me.

OLD OCTOBER

OLD October's purt' nigh gone,
   And the frosts is comin' on
   Little *heavier* every day—
Like our hearts is thataway!
Leaves is changin' overhead
Back from green to gray and red
Brown and yeller, with their stems
Loosenin' on the oaks and e'ms;
And the balance of the trees
Gittin' balder every breeze—
Like the heads we're scratchin' on!
Old October's purt' nigh gone.

I love Old October so,
I can't bear to see her go—
Seems to me like losin' some
Old-home relative er chum—
'Pears like sort o' settin' by
Some old friend 'at sigh by sigh
Was a-passin' out o' sight
Into everlastin' night!

Hickernuts a feller hears
Rattlin' down is more like tears
Drappin' on the leaves below—
I love Old October so!

Can't tell what it is about
Old October knocks me out!—
I sleep well enough at night—
And the blamedest appetite
Ever mortal man possessed,—
Last thing et, it tastes the best!—
Warnuts, butternuts, pawpaws,
'Iles and limbers up my jaws
Fer raal service, sich as new
Pork, spareribs, and sausage, too.—
Yit, fer all, they's somepin' 'bout
Old October knocks me out!

THE TREE-TOAD

"'SCUR'OUS-LIKE," said the tree-toad,
    "I've twittered fer rain all day;
      And I got up soon,
      And hollered tel noon—
    But the sun, hit blazed away,
      Tel I jest clumb down in a crawfish-hole,
      Weary at hart, and sick at soul!

  "Dozed away fer an hour,
    And I tackled the thing ag'in:
      And I sung, and sung,
      Tel I knowed my lung
    Was jest about give in;
      And *then*, thinks I, ef hit don't rain *now*,
      They's nothin' in singin', anyhow!

"Onc't in a while some farmer
　　Would come a-drivin' past;
　　　And he'd hear my cry,
　　　And stop and sigh—
Tel I jest laid back, at last,
　　And I hollered rain tel I thought my th'oat
　　Would bust wide open at ever' note!

"But I *fetched* her!—O *I fetched* her!—
　　'Cause a little while ago,
　　　As I kindo' set,
　　　With one eye shet,
And a-singin' soft and low,
　　A voice drapped down on my fevered brain,
　　A-sayin',—'*Ef you'll jest hush I'll rain!*'"

A BAREFOOT BOY

A BAREFOOT boy! I mark him at his play—
  For May is here once more, and so is he,—
  His dusty trousers, rolled half to the knee,
And his bare ankles grimy, too, as they:
Cross-hatchings of the nettle, in array
  Of feverish stripes, hint vividly to me
  Of woody pathways winding endlessly
Along the creek, where even yesterday
He plunged his shrinking body—gasped and shook—
  Yet called the water "warm," with never lack
Of joy. And so, half enviously I look
  Upon this graceless barefoot and his track,—
  His toe stubbed—ay, his big toe-nail knocked back
Like unto the clasp of an old pocketbook.

A COUNTRY PATHWAY

I COME upon it suddenly, alone—
   A little pathway winding in the weeds
That fringe the roadside; and with dreams my own,
   I wander as it leads.

Full wistfully along the slender way,
   Through summer tan of freckled shade and shine,
I take the path that leads me as it may—
   Its every choice is mine.

A chipmunk, or a sudden-whirring quail,
   Is startled by my step as on I fare—
A garter-snake across the dusty trail
   Glances and—is not there.

Above the arching jimson-weeds flare twos
   And twos of sallow-yellow butterflies,
Like blooms of lorn primroses blowing loose
   When autumn winds arise.

The trail dips—dwindles—broadens then, and lifts
　　Itself astride a cross-road dubiously,
And, from the fennel marge beyond it, drifts
　　Still onward, beckoning me.

And though it needs must lure me mile on mile
　　Out of the public highway, still I go,
My thoughts, far in advance in Indian-file,
　　Allure me even so.

Why, I am as a long-lost boy that went
　　At dusk to bring the cattle to the bars,
And was not found again, though Heaven lent
　　His mother all the stars

With which to seek him through that awful night.
　　O years of nights as vain!—Stars never rise
But well might miss their glitter in the light
　　Of tears in mother-eyes!

So—on, with quickened breaths, I follow still—
　　My avant-courier must be obeyed!
Thus am I led, and thus the path, at will,
　　Invites me to invade

A meadow's precincts, where my daring guide
    Clambers the steps of an old-fashioned stile,
And stumbles down again, the other side,
    To gambol there awhile

In pranks of hide-and-seek, as on ahead
    I see it running, while the clover-stalks
Shake rosy fists at me, as though they said—
    "You dog our country-walks

"And mutilate us with your walking-stick!—
    We will not suffer tamely what you do,
And warn you at your peril,—for we'll sic
    Our bumblebees on you!"

But I smile back, in airy nonchalance,—
    The more determined on my wayward quest,
As some bright memory a moment dawns
    A morning in my breast—

Sending a thrill that hurries me along
    In faulty similes of childish skips,
Enthused with lithe contortions of a song
    Performing on my lips.

In wild meanderings o'er pasture wealth—
    Erratic wanderings through dead'ning-lands,
Where sly old brambles, plucking me by stealth,
    Put berries in my hands:

Or the path climbs a boulder—wades a slough—
    Or, rollicking through buttercups and flags,
Goes gaily dancing o'er a deep bayou
    On old tree-trunks and snags:

Or, at the creek, leads o'er a limpid pool
    Upon a bridge the stream itself has made,
With some Spring-freshet for the mighty tool
    That its foundation laid.

I pause a moment here to bend and muse,
    With dreamy eyes, on my reflection, where
A boat-backed bug drifts on a helpless cruise,
    Or wildly oars the air,

As, dimly seen, the pirate of the brook—
    The pike, whose jaunty hulk denotes his speed—
Swings pivoting about, with wary look
    Of low and cunning greed.

Till, filled with other thought, I turn again
    To where the pathway enters in a realm
Of lordly woodland, under sovereign reign
    Of towering oak and elm.

A puritanic quiet here reviles
    The almost whispered warble from the hedge,
And takes a locust's rasping voice and files
    The silence to an edge.

In such a solitude my somber way
    Strays like a misanthrope within a gloom
Of his own shadows—till the perfect day
    Bursts into sudden bloom,

And crowns a long, declining stretch of space,
    Where King Corn's armies lie with flags unfurled,
And where the valley's dint in Nature's face
    Dimples a smiling world.

And lo! through mists that may not be dispelled,
    I see an old farm homestead, as in dreams,
Where, like a gem in costly setting held,
    The old log cabin gleams.

    . . . .

O darling Pathway! lead me bravely on
    Adown your valley-way, and run before
Among the roses crowding up the lawn
    And thronging at the door,—

And carry up the echo there that shall
    Arouse the drowsy dog, that he may bay
The household out to greet the prodigal
    That wanders home to-day.

A FEW OF THE BIRD-FAMILY

THE Old Bob-white, and Chipbird;
    The Flicker, and Chewink,
    And little hopty-skip bird
Along the river-brink.

The Blackbird, and Snowbird,
    The Chicken-hawk, and Crane;
The glossy old black Crow-bird,
    And Buzzard down the lane.

The Yellowbird, and Redbird,
    The Tomtit, and the Cat;
The Thrush, and that Red*head*-bird
    The rest's all pickin' at!

The Jay-bird, and the Bluebird,
    The Sapsuck, and the Wren—
The Cockadoodle-doo-bird,
    And our old Settin'-hen!

A FULL HARVEST

SEEMS like a feller'd ort'o jes' to-day
   Git down and roll and waller, don't you know,
   In that-air stubble, and flop up and crow,
Seein' sich crops! I'll undertake to say
There're no wheat's ever turned out thataway
Afore this season!—Folks is keerless, though,
   And too fergitful—'caze we'd ort'o show
More thankfulness!—Jes' looky hyonder, hey?—
   And watch that little reaper wadin' thue
That last old yaller hunk o' harvest-ground—
   Jes' natchur'ly a-slicin' it in two
Like honeycomb, and gaumin' it around
   The field—like it had nothin' else to do
   On'y jes' waste it all on me and you!

RIGHT HERE AT HOME

RIGHT here at home, boys, in old Hoosierdom,
    Where strangers allus joke us when they come
    And brag o' *their* old States and interprize—
Yit *settle* here; and 'fore they realize,
They're "hoosier" as the rest of us, and live
Right here at home, boys, with their past fergive'!

Right here at home, boys, is the place, I guess,
Fer me and you and plain old happiness:
We hear the World's lots grander—likely so,—
We'll take the World's word fer it and not go.—
We know *its* ways ain't *our* ways—so we'll stay
Right here at home, boys, where we *know* the way.

Right here at home, boys, where a well-to-do
Man's plenty rich enough—and knows it, too,
And's got a' extry dollar, any time,
To boost a feller up 'at *wants* to climb
And's got the git-up in him to go in
And *git there*, like he purt' nigh allus kin!

Right here at home, boys, is the place fer us!—
Where folks' heart's bigger'n their money-pu's';
And where a *common* feller's jes' as good
As ary other in the neighborhood:
The World at large don't worry you and me
Right here at home, boys, where we ort to be!

Right here at home, boys—jes' right where we air!—
Birds don't sing any sweeter anywhere:
Grass don't grow any greener'n she grows
Across the pastur' where the old path goes,—
All things in ear-shot's purty, er in sight,
Right here at home, boys, ef we *size* 'em right.

Right here at home, boys, where the old home-place
Is sacerd to us as our mother's face,
Jes' as we rickollect her, last she smiled
And kissed us—dyin' so and rickonciled,
Seein' us all at home here—none astray—
Right here at home, boys, where she sleeps to-day.

OLD WINTERS ON THE FARM

I HAVE jest about decided
It 'ud keep a *town-boy* hoppin'
Fer to work all winter, choppin'
Fer a' old fireplace, like *I* did!
Lawz! them old times wuz contrairy!—
    Blame' backbone o' winter, 'peared-like
    Wouldn't break!—and I wuz skeerd-like
Clean on into *Feb'uary!*
    Nothin' ever made me madder
Than fer Pap to stomp in, layin'
On a' extra fore-stick, sayin'
    "Groun'-hog's out and seed his shadder!"

THE OLD HOME BY THE MILL

THIS is "The old Home by the Mill"—fer we still call it so,
    Although the *old mill*, roof and sill, is all gone long ago.
The old home, though, and old folks—and the old spring, and a few
Old cattails, weeds and hartychokes, is left to welcome you!

Here, Marg'et, fetch the man a tin to drink out of! Our spring
Keeps kindo'-sorto' cavin' in, but don't "*taste*" anything!
She's kindo' *agin'*, Marg'et is—"the *old* process," like me,
All ham-stringed up with rhumatiz, and on in seventy-three.

Jes' me and Marg'et lives alone here—like in long ago;
The childern all putt off and gone, and married, don't you know?

One's millin' way out West somewhare; two other
    miller-boys
In Minnyopolis they air; and one's in Illinoise.

The *oldest* gyrl—the first that went—married and died
    right here;
The next lives in Winn's Settlement—for purt' nigh
    thirty year!
And youngest one—was allus fer the old home here—
    but no!—
Her man turns in and packs *her* 'way off to Idyho!

I don't miss them like *Marg'et* does—'cause I got *her*,
    you see;
And when she pines for them—that's 'cause *she's* only
    jes' got *me!*
I laugh, and joke her 'bout it all.—But talkin' sense, I'll
    say,
When she was tuk so bad last Fall, I laughed then t'other
    way!

I hain't so favor'ble impressed 'bout *dyin'*; but ef I
Found I was only second-best when *us two* come to die,
I'd 'dopt the "new process," in full, ef *Marg'et* died, you
    see,—
I'd jes' crawl in my grave and pull the green grass over
    me!

SOMEP'N COMMON-LIKE

SOMEP'N 'at's common-like, and good
And plain, and easy understood;
Somep'n 'at folks like me and you
Kin understand, and relish, too,
And find some sermint in 'at hits
The spot, and sticks and benefits.

We don't need nothin' extry fine;
'Cause, take the run o' minds like mine,
And we'll go more on good horse-sense
Than all your flowery eloquence;
And we'll jedge best of honest acts
By Nature's statement of the facts.

So when you're wantin' to express
Your misery, er happiness,
Er anything 'at's wuth the time
O' telling in plain talk er rhyme—
Jes' sort o' let your subject run
As ef the Lord wuz listenun.

WRITIN' BACK TO THE HOME-FOLKS

MY dear old friends—It jes' beats all,
    The way you write a letter
    So's ever' *last* line beats the *first*,
And ever' *next*-un's better!—
W'y, ever' fool-thing you putt down
    You make so inte*res*tin',
A feller, readin' of 'em all,
    Can't tell which is the *best*-un.

It's all so comfortin' and good,
    'Pears-like I almost *hear* ye
And git more sociabler, you know,
    And hitch my cheer up near ye
And jes' smile on ye like the sun
    Acrosst the whole per-rairies
In Aprile when the thaw's begun
    And country couples marries.

It's all so good-old-fashioned like
   To *talk* jes' like we're *thinkin'*,
Without no hidin' back o' fans
   And giggle-un and winkin',
Ner sizin' how each other's dressed—
   Like some is allus doin'—
"*Is* Marthy Ellen's basque be'n *turned*
   Er shore-enough a new-un!"—

Er "ef Steve's city-friend hain't jes'
   'A *lee*tle kind o' sort o' ' "—
Er "wears them-air blame' eye-glasses
   Jes' 'cause he hadn't ort to?"—
And so straight on, *dad-libitum*,
   Tel all of us feels, *some*way,
Jes' like our "comp'ny" wuz the best
   When we git up to come 'way!

That's why I like *old* friends like you,—
   Jes' 'cause you're so *abidin'*.—
Ef I was built to live "*fer keeps*,"
   My principul residin'
Would be amongst the folks 'at kep'
   Me allus *thinkin'* of 'em
And sort o' eechin' all the time
   To tell 'em how I love 'em.—

Sich folks, you know, I jes' love so
  I wouldn't live without 'em,
Er couldn't even drap asleep
  But what I *dreamp'* about 'em,—
And ef we minded God, I guess
  We'd *all* love one another
Jes' like one famb'ly,—me and Pap
  And Madaline and Mother.

AT "THE LITERARY"

FOLKS in town, I reckon, thinks
    They git all the fun they air
    Runnin' loose 'round!—but, 'y jinks!
We' got fun, and fun to spare,
Right out here amongst the ash-
    And oak-timber ever'where!
Some folks else kin cut a dash
    'Sides town-people, don't fergit!—
'Specially in *winter*-time,
    When they's snow, and roads is fit.
In them circumstances I'm
    Resig-nated to my lot—
    Which putts me in mind o' what
        'S called "The Literary."

Us folks in the country sees
    Lots o' fun!—Take spellin'-school;
Er ole hoe-down jamborees;
    Er revivals; er ef you'll

Tackle taffy-pullin's you
Kin git fun, and quite a few!—
   Same with huskin's. But all these
Kind o' frolics they hain't new
By a hunderd year' er two,
   Cipher on it as you please!
But I'll tell you what I jest
Think walks over all the rest—
Anyway it suits *me* best,—
   That's "The Literary."

First they started it—" 'y gee!"
   Thinks-says-I, "this settle-ment
'S gittin' too high-toned fer me!"
   But when all begin to jine,
   And I heerd *Izory* went,
     I jest kind o' drapped in line,
Like you've seen some sandy, thin,
   Scrawny shoat putt fer the crick
   Down some pig-trail through the thick
Spice-bresh, where the whole drove's been
'Bout six weeks 'fore he gits in!—
"Can't tell nothin'," I-says-ee,
" 'Bout it tel you go and see
   Their blame 'Literary'!"

Very first night I was there
   I was 'p'inted to be what
They call "Critic"—so's a fair
   And square jedgment could be got
     On the pieces 'at was read,
And on the debate,—"Which air
   Most destructive element,
     Fire er worter?" Then they hed
   Compositions on "Content,"
"Death," and "Botany"; and Tomps
He read one on "Dreenin' Swamps"
I p'nounced the boss, and said,
"*So* fur, 'at's the best thing read
     In yer 'Literary'!"

Then they *sung* some—tel I called
   Order, and got back ag'in
In the critic's cheer, and hauled
   All o' the p'formers in:—
Mandy Brizendine read one
   I fergit; and Doc's was "Thought";
And Sarepty's, hern was "None
   Air Denied 'at Knocks"; and Daut—
Fayette Strawnse's little niece—
She got up and spoke a piece:

Then Izory she read hern—
"Best thing in the whole concern,"
I-says-ee; "now le' 's adjourn
    This-here 'Literary'!"

They was some contendin'—yit
    We broke up in harmony.
Road outside as white as grit,
    And as slick as slick could be!—
I'd fetched 'Zory in my sleigh,—
And I had a heap to say,
    Drivin' back—in fact, I driv
'Way around the old north way,
    Where the Daubenspeckses live.
'Zory allus—'fore that night—
Never 'peared to feel jest right
In my company.—You see,
On'y thing on earth saved me
    Was that "Literary"!

DOWN TO THE CAPITAL

I' BE'N down to the Capital at Washington, D. C.,
　　Where Congerss meets and passes on the pensions ort
　　　　to be
Allowed to old one-legged chaps, like me, 'at sence the
　　war
Don't wear their pants in pairs at all—and yit how proud
　　we are!

Old Flukens, from our deestrick, jes' turned in and tuck
　　and made
Me stay with him whilse I was there; and longer 'at I
　　stayed
The more I kep' a-wantin' jes' to kind o' git away,
And yit a-feelin' sociabler with Flukens ever' day.

You see I'd got the idy—and I guess most folks agrees—
'At men as rich as him, you know, kin do jes' what they
　　please;
A man worth stacks o' money, and a Congerssman and
　　all,
And livin' in a buildin' bigger'n Masonic Hall!

Now mind, I'm not a-faultin' Fluke—he made his money square:
We both was Forty-niners, and both bu'sted gittin' there;
I weakened and onwindlassed, and he stuck and stayed and made
His millions; don't know what *I'm* worth untel my pension's paid.

But I was goin' to tell you—er a-ruther goin' to try
To tell you how he's livin' now: gas burnin' mighty nigh
In ever' room about the house; and ever' night about,
Some blame reception goin' on, and money goin' out.

They's people there from all the world—jes' ever' kind 'at lives,
Injuns and all! and Senators, and Ripresentatives;
And girls, you know, jes' dressed in gauze and roses I *de*clare,
And even old men shamblin' round and a-waltzin' with 'em there!

And bands a-tootin' circus-tunes, 'way in some other room
Jes' chokin' full o' hothouse plants and pinies and perfume;
And fountains, squirtin' stiddy all the time; and statutes, made
Out o' puore marble, 'peared-like, sneakin' round there in the shade.

And Fluke he coaxed and begged and pled with *me* to
  take a hand
And sashay in amongst 'em—crutch and all, you under-
  stand;
But when I said how tired I was, and made fer open air,
He follered, and tel five o'clock we set a-talkin' there.

"My God!" says he—Fluke says to me, "I'm tireder'n
  you;
Don't putt up yer tobacker tel you give a man a chew.
Set back a leetle furder in the shadder—that'll do;
I'm tireder'n you, old man; I'm tireder'n you.

"You see that-air old dome," says he, "humped up ag'inst
  the sky?
It's grand, first time you see it; but it changes, by and by,
And then it stays jes' thataway—jes' anchored high and
  dry
Betwixt the sky up yender and the achin' of yer eye.

"Night's purty; not so purty, though, as what it ust to be
When my first wife was livin'. You remember her?"
  says he.
I nodded-like, and Fluke went on, "I wonder now ef she
Knows where I am—and what I am—and what I ust to
  be?

"That band in there!—I ust to think 'at music couldn't
    wear
A feller out the way it does; but that ain't music there—
That's jes' a' *imitation*, and like ever'thing, I swear,
I hear, er see, er tetch, er taste, er tackle anywhere!

"It's all jes' *artificial*, this-'ere high-priced life of ours;
The theory, *it's* sweet enough, tel it saps down and sours.
They's no *home* left, ner *ties* o' home about it. By the
    powers,
The whole thing's artificialer'n artificial flowers!

"And all I want, and could lay down and *sob* fer, is to
    know
The homely things of homely life; fer instance, jes' to go
And set down by the kitchen stove—Lord! that 'u'd rest
    me so,—
Jes' set there, like I ust to do, and laugh and joke, you
    know.

"Jes' set there, like I ust to do," says Fluke, a-startin' in,
'Peared-like, to say the whole thing over to hisse'f ag'in;
Then stopped and turned, and kind o' coughed, and
    stooped and fumbled fer
Somepin' o' 'nuther in the grass—I guess his handker-
    cher.

Well, sence I'm back from Washington, where I left
   Fluke a-still
A-leggin' fer me, heart and soul, on that-air pension bill,
I've half-way struck the notion, when I think o' wealth
   and sich,
They's nothin' much patheticker'n jes' a-bein' rich!

THE OLD MAN AND JIM

OLD man never had much to say—
    'Ceptin' to Jim,—
  And Jim was the wildest boy he had—
And the old man jes' wrapped up in him!
Never heerd him speak but once
    Er twice in my life,—and first time was
      When the army broke out, and Jim he went,
The old man backin' him, fer three months;
And all 'at I heerd the old man say
Was, jes' as we turned to start away,—
    "Well, good-by, Jim:
      Take keer of yourse'f!"

'Peared-like, he was more satisfied
    Jes' *lookin'* at Jim
And likin' him all to hisse'f-like, see?—
    'Cause he was jes' wrapped up in him!
And over and over I mind the day
The old man come and stood round in the way
    While we was drillin', a-watchin' Jim—
And down at the deepo a-heerin' him say,

"Well, good-by, Jim:
   Take keer of yourse'f!"

Never was nothin' about the *farm*
   Disting'ished Jim;
Neighbors all ust to wonder why
   The old man 'peared wrapped up in him:
But when Cap. Biggler he writ back
   'At Jim was the bravest boy we had
In the whole dern rigiment, white er black,
   And his fightin' good as his farmin' bad—
'At he had led, with a bullet clean
     Bored through his thigh, and carried the flag
Through the bloodiest battle you ever seen,—
The old man wound up a letter to him
   'At Cap. read to us, 'at said : "Tell Jim
   Good-by,
      And take keer of hisse'f."

Jim come home jes' long enough
   To take the whim
'At he'd like to go back in the calvery—
   And the old man jes' wrapped up in him!
Jim 'lowed 'at he'd had sich luck afore,
Guessed he'd tackle her three years more.
And the old man give him a colt he'd raised,
And follered him over to Camp Ben Wade,

And laid around fer a week er so,
Watchin' Jim on dress-parade—
Tel finally he rid away,
And last he heerd was the old man say,—
   "Well, good-by, Jim:
      Take keer of yourse'f!"

Tuk the papers, the old man did,
   A-watchin' fer Jim—
Fully believin' he'd make his mark
   Some way—jes' wrapped up in him!—
And many a time the word 'u'd come
'At stirred him up like the tap of a drum—
At Petersburg, fer instunce, where
Jim rid right into their cannons there,
And *tuk* 'em, and p'inted 'em t'other way,
And socked it home to the boys in gray
   As they scooted fer timber, and on and on—
Jim a lieutenant, and one arm gone,
And the old man's words in his mind all day,—
   "Well, good-by, Jim:
      Take keer of yourse'f!"

Think of a private, now, perhaps,
   We'll say like Jim,
'At's clumb clean up to the shoulder-straps—
   And the old man jes' wrapped up in him!

Think of him—with the war plum' through,
And the glorious old Red-White-and-Blue
A-laughin' the news down over Jim,
And the old man, bendin' over him—
The surgeon turnin' away with tears
'At hadn't leaked fer years and years,
As the hand of the dyin' boy clung to
His father's, the old voice in his ears,—
    "Well, good-by, Jim:
        Take keer of yourse'f!"

HERR WEISER

HERR WEISER!—Threescore-years-and-
ten,—
A hale white rose of his countrymen,
Transplanted here in the Hoosier loam,
And blossomy as his German home—
As blossomy and as pure and sweet
As the cool green glen of his calm retreat,
Far withdrawn from the noisy town
Where trade goes clamoring up and down,
Whose fret and fever, and stress and strife,
May not trouble his tranquil life!

Breath of rest, what a balmy gust!—
Quit of the city's heat and dust,
Jostling down by the winding road,
Through the orchard ways of his quaint abode.—
Tether the horse, as we onward fare
Under the pear-trees trailing there,
And thumping the wooden bridge at night
With lumps of ripeness and lush delight,

Till the stream, as it maunders on till dawn,
Is powdered and pelted and smiled upon.

Herr Weiser, with his wholesome face,
And the gentle blue of his eyes, and grace
Of unassuming honesty,
Be there to welcome you and me!
And what though the toil of the farm be stopped
And the tireless plans of the place be dropped,
While the prayerful master's knees are set
In beds of pansy and mignonette
And lily and aster and columbine,
Offered in love, as yours and mine?—

What, but a blessing of kindly thought,
Sweet as the breath of forget-me-not!—
What, but a spirit of lustrous love
White as the aster he bends above!—
What, but an odorous memory
Of the dear old man, made known to me
In days demanding a help like his,—
As sweet as the life of the lily is—
As sweet as the soul of a babe, bloom-wise
Born of a lily in paradise.

MARTHY ELLEN

THEY'S nothin' in the name to strike
   A feller more'n common like!
   'Taint liable to git no praise
Ner nothin' like it nowadays;
An' yit that name o' her'n is jest
As purty as the purtiest—
And more'n that, I'm here to say
I'll live a-thinkin' thataway
        And die fer Marthy Ellen!

It may be I was prejudust
In favor of it from the fust—
'Cause I kin ricollect jest how
We met, and hear her mother now
A-callin' of her down the road—
And, aggervatin' little toad!—
I see her now, jest sort o' half-
Way disapp'inted, turn and laugh
        And mock her—"Marthy Ellen!"

Our people never had no fuss,
And yit they never tuck to us;
We neighbered back and foreds some;
Until they see she liked to come
To our house—and me and her
Was jest together ever'whur
And all the time—and when they'd see
That I liked her and she liked me,
   They'd holler "Marthy Ellen!"

When we growed up, and they shet down
On me and her a-runnin' roun'
Together, and her father said
He'd never leave her nary red,
So he'p him, ef she married me,
And so on—and her mother she
Jest agged the gyrl, and said she 'lowed
She'd ruther see her in her shroud,
   I *writ* to Marthy Ellen—

That is, I kind o' tuck my pen
In hand, and stated whur and when
The undersigned would be that night,
With two good hosses, saddled right
Fer lively travelin', in case
Her folks 'ud like to jine the race.

She sent the same note back, and writ
"The rose is red!" right under it—
    "Your'n allus, Marthy Ellen."

That's all, I reckon—Nothin' more
To tell but what you've heerd afore—
The same old story, sweeter though
Fer all the trouble, don't you know.
Old-fashioned name! and yit it's jest
As purty as the purtiest;
And more'n that, I'm here to say
I'll live a-thinkin' thataway,
    And die fer Marthy Ellen!

AN OLD MAN'S MEMORY

THE delights of our childhood is soon passed
    away,
  And our gloryus youth it departs,—
And yit, dead and burried, they's blossoms of May
  Ore theyr medderland graves in our harts.
So, friends of my barefooted days on the farm,
  Whether truant in city er not,
God prosper you same as He's prosperin' me,
  Whilse your past hain't despised er forgot.

Oh! they's nothin', at morn, that's as grand unto me
  As the glorys of Natchur so fare,—
With the Spring in the breeze, and the bloom in the trees,
  And the hum of the bees ev'rywhare!
The green in the woods, and the birds in the boughs,
  And the dew spangled over the fields;
And the bah of the sheep and the bawl of the cows
  And the call from the house to your meals!

Then ho! fer your brekfast! and ho! fer the toil
    That waiteth alike man and beast!
Oh! it's soon with my team I'll be turnin' up soil,
    Whilse the sun shoulders up in the East
Ore the tops of the ellums and beeches and oaks,
    To smile his Godspeed on the plow,
And the furry and seed, and the Man in his need,
    And the joy of the swet of his brow!

WORTERMELON TIME

OLD wortermelon time is a-comin' round ag'in,
    And they ain't no man a-livin' any tickleder'n
        me,
Fer the way I hanker after wortermelons is a sin—
    Which is the why and wharefore, as you can plainly
        see.

Oh! it's in the sandy soil wortermelons does the best,
    And it's thare they'll lay and waller in the sunshine
        and the dew
Tel they wear all the green streaks clean off of theyr
        breast;
    And you bet I ain't a-findin' any fault with them; air
        you?

They ain't no better thing in the vegetable line;
    And they don't need much 'tendin', as ev'ry farmer
        knows;
And when theyr ripe and ready fer to pluck from the
        vine,
    I want to say to you theyr the best fruit that grows.

It's some likes the yeller-core, and some likes the red,
    And it's some says "The Little Californy" is the best;
But the sweetest slice of all I ever wedged in my head,
    Is the old "Edingburg Mounting-sprout," of the West.

You don't want no punkins nigh your wortermelon vines—
    'Cause, some-way-another, they'll spile your melons, shore;—
I've seed 'em taste like punkins, from the core to the rines,
    Which may be a fact you have heerd of before.

But your melons that's raised right and 'tended to with care,
    You can walk around amongst 'em with a parent's pride and joy,
And thump 'em on the heads with as fatherly a air
    As ef each one of them was your little girl er boy.

I joy in my hart jest to hear that rippin' sound
    When you split one down the back and jolt the halves in two,
And the friends you love the best is gethered all around—
    And you says unto your sweethart, "Oh, here's the core fer you!"

And I like to slice 'em up in big pieces fer 'em all,
  Espeshally the childern, and watch theyr high delight
As one by one the rines with theyr pink notches falls,
  And they holler fer some more, with unquenched appetite.

Boys takes to it natchurl, and I like to see 'em eat—
  A slice of wortermelon's like a frenchharp in theyr hands,
And when they "saw" it through theyr mouth sich music can't be beat—
  'Cause it's music both the sperit and the stummick understands.

Oh, they's more in wortermelons than the purty-colored meat,
  And the overflowin' sweetness of the worter squshed betwixt
The up'ard and the down'ard motions of a feller's teeth,
  And it's the taste of ripe old age and juicy childhood mixed.

Fer I never taste a melon but my thoughts flies away
  To the summertime of youth; and again I see the dawn,
And the fadin' afternoon of the long summer day,
  And the dusk and dew a-fallin', and the night a-comin' on.

And thare's the corn around us, and the lispin' leaves and trees,
    And the stars a-peekin' down on us as still as silver mice,
And us boys in the wortermelons on our hands and knees,
    And the new-moon hangin' ore us like a yeller-cored slice.

Oh! it's wortermelon time is a-comin' round ag'in,
    And they ain't no man a-livin' any tickleder'n me,
Fer the way I hanker after wortermelons is a sin—
    Which is the why and wharefore, as you can plainly see.

WHEN THE FROST IS ON THE PUNKIN

WHEN the frost is on the punkin and the fodder's in the shock,
And you hear the kyouck and gobble of the struttin' turkey-cock,
And the clackin' of the guineys, and cluckin' of the hens,
And the rooster's hallylooyer as he tiptoes on the fence;
O, it's then's the times a feller is a-feelin' at his best,
With the risin' sun to greet him from a night of peaceful rest,
As he leaves the house, bare-headed, and goes out to feed the stock,
When the frost is on the punkin and the fodder's in the shock.

They's something kindo' harty-like about the atmusfere
When the heat of summer's over and the coolin' fall is here—
Of course we miss the flowers, and the blossoms on the trees,
And the mumble of the hummin'-birds and the buzzin' of the bees;

But the air's so appetizin'; and the landscape through the haze
Of a crisp and sunny morning of the airly autumn days
Is a pictur' that no painter has the colorin' to mock—
When the frost is on the punkin and the fodder's in the shock

The husky, rusty russel of the tossels of the corn,
And the raspin' of the tangled leaves, as golden as the morn;
The stubble in the furries—kindo' lonesome-like, but still
A-preachin' sermuns to us of the barns they growed to fill;
The strawstack in the medder, and the reaper in the shed;
The hosses in theyr stalls below—the clover overhead!—
O, it sets my hart a-clickin' like the tickin' of a clock,
When the frost is on the punkin and the fodder's in the shock!

Then your apples all is getherd, and the ones a feller keeps
Is poured around the celler-floor in red and yeller heaps;
And your cider-makin' 's over, and your wimmern-folks is through
With their mince and apple-butter, and theyr souse and saussage, too! . . .

I don't know how to tell it—but ef sich a thing could be
As the Angels wantin' boardin', and they'd call around on *me*—
I'd want to 'commodate 'em—all the whole-indurin' flock—
When the frost is on the punkin and the fodder's in the shock!

AUGUST

A DAY of torpor in the sullen heat
    Of Summer's passion: In the sluggish stream
    The panting cattle lave their lazy feet,
With drowsy eyes, and dream.

Long since the winds have died, and in the sky
   There lives no cloud to hint of Nature's grief;
The sun glares ever like an evil eye,
   And withers flower and leaf.

Upon the gleaming harvest-field remote
   The thresher lies deserted, like some old
Dismantled galleon that hangs afloat
   Upon a sea of gold.

The yearning cry of some bewildered bird.
   Above an empty nest, and truant boys
Along the river's shady margin heard—
   A harmony of noise—

A melody of wrangling voices blent
   With liquid laughter, and with rippling calls
Of piping lips and trilling echoes sent
   To mimic waterfalls.

And through the hazy veil the atmosphere
   Has draped about the gleaming face of Day,
The sifted glances of the sun appear
   In splinterings of spray.

The dusty highway, like a cloud of dawn,
   Trails o'er the hillside, and the passer-by,
A tired ghost in misty shroud, toils on
   His journey to the sky.

And down across the valley's drooping sweep,
   Withdrawn to farthest limit of the glade,
The forest stands in silence, drinking deep
   Its purple wine of shade.

The gossamer floats up on phantom wing;
   The sailor-vision voyages the skies
And carries into chaos everything
   That freights the weary eyes:

Till, throbbing on and on, the pulse of heat
   Increases—reaches—passes fever's height,
And Day sinks into slumber, cool and sweet,
   Within the arms of Night.

BACK FROM TOWN

OLD friends allus is the best,
    Halest-like and heartiest:
    Knowed us first, and don't allow
We're so blame much better now!
They was standin' at the bars
When we grabbed "the kivvered kyars"
And lit out fer town, to make
Money—and that old mistake!

We thought then the world we went
Into beat "The Settlement,"
And the friends 'at we'd make there
Would beat any anywhere!—
And they *do*—fer that's their biz:
They beat all the friends they is—
'Cept the raal old friends like you
'At staid home, like *I'd* ort to!

W'y, of all the good things yit
I ain't shet of, is to quit

Business, and git back to sheer
These old comforts waitin' here—
These old friends; and these old hands
'At a feller understands;
These old winter nights, and old
Young-folks chased in out the cold!

Sing "Hard Times'll come ag'in
No More!" and neighbors all jine in!
Here's a feller come from town
Wants that-air old fiddle down
From the chimbly!—Git the floor
Cleared fer one cowtillion more!—
It's poke the kitchen fire, says he,
And shake a friendly leg with me!

A DREAM OF AUTUMN

MELLOW hazes, lowly trailing
    Over wood and meadow, veiling
    Somber skies, with wild-fowl sailing
  Sailor-like to foreign lands;
And the north-wind overleaping
Summer's brink, and flood-like sweeping
Wrecks of roses where the weeping-
  Willows wring their helpless hands.

Flared, like Titan torches flinging
Flakes of flame and embers, springing
From the vale, the trees stand swinging
  In the moaning atmosphere;
While in dead'ning lands the lowing
Of the cattle, sadder growing,
Fills the sense to overflowing
  With the sorrow of the year.

Sorrowfully, yet the sweeter
Sings the brook in rippled meter
Under boughs that lithely teeter

Lorn birds, answering from the shores
Through the viny, shady-shiny
Interspaces, shot with tiny
Flying motes that fleck the winy
   Wave-engraven sycamores.

Fields of ragged stubble, wrangled
With rank weeds, and shocks of tangled
Corn, with crests like rent plumes dangled
   Over Harvest's battle-plain;
And the sudden whir and whistle
Of the quail that, like a missile,
Whizzes over thorn and thistle,
   And, a missile, drops again.

Muffled voices, hid in thickets
Where the redbird stops to stick its
Ruddy beak betwixt the pickets
   Of the truant's rustic trap;
And the sound of laughter ringing
Where, within the wild vine swinging,
Climb Bacchante's schoolmates, flinging
   Purple clusters in her lap.

Rich as wine, the sunset flashes
Round the tilted world, and dashes
Up the sloping west, and splashes
   Red foam over sky and sea—
Till my dream of Autumn, paling
In the splendor all-prevailing,
Like a sallow leaf goes sailing
   Down the silence solemnly.

THE BOYS

WHERE are they?—the friends of my child-
         hood enchanted—
    The clear, laughing eyes looking back in
  my own,
And the warm, chubby fingers my palms have so wanted,
    As when we raced over
              Pink pastures of clover,
    And mocked the quail's whir and the bumblebee's
  drone?

Have the breezes of time blown their blossomy faces
    Forever adrift down the years that are flown?
Am I never to see them romp back to their places,
    Where over the meadow,
              In sunshine and shadow,
    The meadow-larks trill, and the bumblebees drone?

Where are they? Ah! dim in the dust lies the clover;
    The whippoorwill's call has a sorrowful tone,
And the dove's—I have wept at it over and over;—
    I want the glad lustre
              Of youth, and the cluster
    Of faces asleep where the bumblebees drone!

THE FIRST BLUEBIRD

JEST rain and snow! and rain again!
    And dribble! drip! and blow!
    Then snow! and thaw! and slush! and then
Some more rain and snow!

This morning I was 'most afeard
    To *wake* up—when, I jing!
I seen the sun shine out and heerd
    The first bluebird of Spring!—
Mother she'd raised the winder some;—
And in acrost the orchurd come,
    Soft as a' angel's wing,
A breezy, treesy, beesy hum,
    Too sweet fer anything!

The winter's shroud was rent apart—
    The sun bu'st forth in glee,—
And when *that bluebird* sung, my hart
    Hopped out o' bed with me!

TOWN AND COUNTRY

THEY'S a predjudice allus 'twixt country and
    town
  Which I wisht in my hart wasent so.
You take *city* people, jest square up and down,
  And they're mighty good people to know:
And whare's better people a-livin', to-day,
  Than us in the *country?* —Yit good
As both of us is, we're divorsed, you might say,
  And won't compermise when we could!

Now as nigh into town fer yer Pap, ef you please,
  Is what's called the sooburbs.—Fer thare
You'll at least ketch a whiff of the breeze and a sniff
  Of the breth of wild-flowrs ev'rywhare.
They's room fer the childern to play, and grow, too—
  And to roll in the grass, er to climb
Up a tree and rob nests, like they *ortent* to do,
  But they'll do *anyhow* ev'ry time!

My Son-in-law said, when he lived in the town,
    He jest natchurly pined, night and day,
Fer a sight of the woods, er a acre of ground
    Whare the trees wasent all cleared away!
And he says to me onc't, whilse a-visitin' us
    On the farm, "It's not strange, I declare,
That we can't coax you folks, without raisin' a fuss,
    To come to town, visitin' thare!"

And says I, "Then git back whare you sorto' *belong*—
    And *Madaline*, too,—and yer three
Little childern," says I, "that don't know a bird-song,
    Ner a hawk from a chicky-dee-dee!
Git back," I-says-I, "to the blue of the sky
    And the green of the fields, and the shine
Of the sun, with a laugh in yer voice and yer eye
    As harty as Mother's and mine!"

Well—long-and-short of it,—he's compermised *some*—
    He's moved in the sooburbs.—And now
They don't haf to coax, when they want us to come,
    'Cause we turn in and go *anyhow!*
Fer thare—well, they's room fer the songs and purfume
    Of the grove and the old orchurd-ground,
And they's room fer the childern out thare, and they's room
    Fer theyr Gran'pap to waller 'em round!

DECORATION DAY ON THE PLACE

IT'S lonesome—sorto' lonesome,—it's a *Sund'y-day*,
    to me,
It 'pears-like—more'n any day I nearly ever see!—
Yit, with the Stars and Stripes above, a-flutterin' in the
    air,
On ev'ry Soldier's grave I'd love to lay a lily thare.

They say, though, Decoration Day is giner'ly observed
'Most *ev'rywhares*— espeshally by soldier-boys that's
    served.—
But me and Mother's never went—we seldom git
    away,—
In p'int o' fact, we're *allus* home on *Decoration Day*.

They say the old boys marches through the streets in
    colum's grand,
A-follerin' the old war-tunes they're playin' on the
    band—
And citizuns all jinin' in—and little childern, too—
All marchin', under shelter of the old Red White and
    Blue.—

With roses! roses! roses!—ev'rybody in the town!—
And crowds o' little girls in white, jest fairly loaded down!—
Oh! don't THE BOYS know it, from theyr camp acrost the hill? —
Don't they see theyr com'ards comin' and the old flag wavin' still?

Oh! can't they hear the bugul and the rattle of the drum?—
Ain't they no way under heavens they can rickollect us some?
Ain't they no way we can coax 'em, through the roses, jest to say
They know that ev'ry day on earth's theyr Decoration Day?

We've tried that—me and Mother,—whare Elias takes his rest,
In the orchurd—in his uniform, and hands acrost his brest,
And the flag he died fer, smilin' and a-ripplin' in the breeze
Above his grave—and over that,—*the robin in the trees!*

And *yit* it's lonesome—lonesome!—It's a *Sund'y-day*, to *me*,
It 'pears-like—more'n any day I nearly ever see!—
Still, with the Stars and Stripes above, a-flutterin' in the air,
On ev'ry Soldier's grave I'd love to lay a lily thare.

THE OLD BAND

IT'S mighty good to git back to the old town, shore,
Considerin' I've be'n away twenty year and more.
Sence I moved then to Kansas, of course I see a change,
A-comin' back, and notice things that's new to me and strange;
Especially at evening when yer new band-fellers meet,
In fancy uniforms and all, and play out on the street—
. . . What's come of old Bill Lindsey and the Saxhorn fellers—say?
      I want to hear the *old* band play.

What's come of Eastman, and Nat Snow? And where's War Barnett at?
And Nate and Bony Meek; Bill Hart; Tom Richa'son and that
Air brother of him played the drum as twic't as big as Jim;
And old Hi Kerns, the carpenter—say, what's become o' him?

I make no doubt yer *new band* now's a *competenter* band,
And plays their music more by note than what they play
    by hand,
And stylisher and grander tunes; but somehow—*any-
    way*,
    I want to hear the *old* band play.

Sich tunes as "John Brown's Body" and "Sweet Alice,"
    don't you know;
And "The Camels Is A-Comin'," and "John Anderson,
    My Jo";
And a dozen others of 'em—"Number Nine" and
    "Number 'Leven"
Was favo-*rites* that fairly made a feller dream o'
    Heaven.
And when the boys 'u'd saranade, I've laid so still in bed
I've even heerd the locus'-blossoms droppin' on the shed
When "Lily Dale," er "Hazel Dell," had sobbed and
    died away—
    . . . I want to hear the *old* band play.

Yer *new* band ma'by beats it, but the *old band*'s what I
    said—
It allus 'peared to kind o' chord with somepin' in my
    head;

And, whilse I'm no musicianer, when my blame' eyes is
  jes'
Nigh drownded out, and Mem'ry squares her jaws and
  sort o' says
She *won't* ner *never will* fergit, I want to jes' turn in
And take and light right out o' here and git back West
  ag'in
And *stay* there, when I git there, where I never haf' to
  say
      I want to hear the *old* band play.

"LAST CHRISTMAS WAS A YEAR AGO"

THE OLD LADY SPEAKS

LAST Christmas was a year ago,
   Says I to David, I-says-I,
   "We're goin' to morning service, so
You hitch up right away: I'll try
To tell the girls jes' what to do
Fer dinner.—We'll be back by two."
I didn't wait to hear what he
Would more'n like say back to me,
But banged the stable door and flew
Back to the house, jes' plumb chilled through.

Cold! *Wooh!* how cold it was! My-oh!
Frost flyin', and the air, you know,
"Jes' sharp enough," heerd David swear,
"To shave a man and cut his hair!"
And blow and blow! and snow and snow!—
   Where it had drifted 'long the fence
And 'crost the road,—some places, though,
Jes' swep' clean to the gravel, so

The goin' was as bad fer sleighs
As 'twas fer wagons,—and both ways,
'Twixt snow-drifts and the bare ground, I've
Jes' wundered we got through alive;
 I hain't saw nothin', 'fore er sence,
'At beat it anywheres, I know—
Last Christmas was a year ago.

And David said, as we set out,
'At Christmas services was 'bout
  As cold and wuthless kind o' love
    To offer up as he knowed of;
And as fer him, he railly thought
  'At the Good Bein' up above
Would think more of us—as He ought—
A-stayin' home on sich a day,
And thankin' of Him thataway!
And jawed on, in an undertone,
'Bout leavin' Lide and Jane alone
There on the place, and me not there
To oversee 'em, and p'pare
The stuffin' fer the turkey, and
The sass and all, you understand.

I've allus managed David by
Jes' sayin' *nothin'*. That was why
He'd chased Lide's beau away—'cause Lide
She'd allus take up Perry's side
When David tackled him; and so,
Last Christmas was a year ago,—
Er ruther, 'bout *a week afore*,—

   David and Perry'd quarr'l'd about
Some tom-fool argyment, you know,
   And Pap told him to "Jes' git out
O' there, and not to come no more,
And, when he went, to shet the door!"
And as he passed the winder, we
Saw Perry, white as white could be,
March past, onhitch his hoss, and light
A see-gyar, and lope out o' sight.
Then Lide she come to me and cried!

   And I said nothin'—was no need.
And yit, you know, that man jes' got
Right out o' there's ef he'd be'n shot,
   P'tendin' he must go and feed
The stock er somepin'. Then I tried
To git the pore girl pacified.

But, gittin' back to—where was we?—
Oh, yes!—where David lectered me
All way to meetin', high and low,
Last Christmas was a year ago:
Fer all the awful cold, they was
A fair attendunce; mostly, though,
The crowd was 'round the stoves, you see,
Thawin' their heels and scrougin' us.

 Ef 't 'adn't be'n fer the old Squire
Givin' *his* seat to us, as in
We stomped, a-fairly perishin',
 And David could 'a' got no fire,
He'd jes' 'a' drapped there in his tracks:
 And Squire, as I was tryin' to yit
Make room fer him, says, "No; the fac's
 Is, *I* got to git up and git
'*Ithout* no preachin'. Jes' got word—
Trial fer life—can't be deferred!"
And out he putt!

. . . . . . And all way through
The sermont—and a long one, too—
I couldn't he'p but think o' Squire
And us changed round so, and admire
His gintle ways,—to give his warm
Bench up, and have to face the storm.
And when I noticed David he

Was needin' jabbin'—I thought best
To kind o' sort o' let him rest:
'Peared-like he slep' so peacefully!
And then I thought o' home, and how
And what the gyrls was doin' now,
And kind o' prayed, 'way in my breast,
And breshed away a tear er two
As David waked, and church was through.

By time we'd "howdyed" round and shuck
Hands with neighbers, must 'a' tuck
A half hour longer: ever' one
A-sayin' "Christmas gift!" afore
David er me—so we got none!
But David warmed up, more and more,
And got so jokey-like, and had
His sperits up, and 'peared so glad,
I whispered to him, "S'pose you ast
A passel of 'em come and eat
Their dinners with us. Gyrls's got
A full-and-plenty fer the lot
And all their kin!" So David passed
The invite round: and ever' seat
In ever' wagon-bed and sleigh
Was jes' packed, as we rode away,—
The young folks, mil'd er so along,
A-strikin' up a sleighin'-song,

Tel David laughed and yelled, you know,
And jes' whirped up and sent the snow
   And gravel flyin' thick and fast—
Last Christmas was a year ago.
W'y, that-air seven-mil'd ja'nt we come—
Jes' seven mil'd scant from church to home—
It didn't 'pear, *that* day, to be
Much furder railly 'n 'bout *three!*

But I was purty squeamish by
The time home hove in sight and I
See two vehickles standin' there
Already. So says I, "*Prepare!*"
All to myse'f. And presently
David he sobered; and says he,
  "Hain't that-air Squire Hanch's old
Buggy," he says, "and claybank mare?"
  Says I, "Le' 's git in out the cold—
   Your company's nigh 'bout froze!" He says,
"Whose sleigh's that-air, a-standin' there?"
   Says I, "It's no odds *whose*—*you* jes'
Drive to the house and let us out,
'Cause we're jes' *freezin'*, nigh about!"
  Well, David swung up to the door,
And out we piled. And first I heerd
  Jane's voice, then *Lide's*,—I thought afore
   I reached that gyrl I'd jes' die, shore;

And *when* I reached her, wouldn't keered
　　Much ef I had, I was so glad,
A-kissin' her through my green veil,
　　And jes' excitin' her so bad,
　　　'At *she* broke down *herse'f*—and Jane,
　　　She cried—and we all hugged again.
And *David?*—David jes' turned pale!—
　　Looked at the gyrls, and then at me,
Then at the open door—and then—
　　"Is old Squire Hanch in there?" says he.
The old Squire suddenly stood in
The doorway, with a sneakin' grin.
"Is Perry Anders in there, too?"
Says David, limberin' all through,
As Lide and me both grabbed him, and
Perry stepped out and waved his hand
And says, "Yes, Pap." And David jes'
Stooped and kissed Lide, and says, "I guess
Yer *mother's* much to blame as you.
Ef *she* kin resk him, I kin too!"

　　The dinner we had then hain't no
Bit better'n the one to-day
'At we'll have fer 'em. Hear some sleigh
A-jinglin' now. David, fer *me*,
I wish you'd jes' go out and see
Ef they're in sight yit. It jes' does

Me good to think, in times like these,
Lide's done so well. And David, he's
More tractabler'n what he was—
   Last Christmas was a year ago.

FESSLER'S BEES

"TALKIN' 'bout yer bees," says Ike,
    Speakin' slow and ser'ous-like,
    "D' ever tell you 'bout old 'Bee'—
Old 'Bee' Fessler?" Ike says-he!
"Might call him a *bee-expert*,
    When it come to handlin' bees,—
Roll the sleeves up of his shirt
    And wade in amongst the trees
        Where a swarm 'u'd settle, and—
Blam'est man on top of dirt!
    Rake 'em with his naked hand
Right back in the hive ag'in,
    Jes' as easy as you please!
    Nary bee 'at split the breeze
Ever jabbed a stinger in
Old 'Bee' Fessler—jes' in fun,
Er in *airnest*—nary one!—
Couldn't agg one *on* to, nuther,
Ary one way er the other!

"Old 'Bee' Fessler," Ike says-he,
"Made a speshyality
Jes' o' bees; and built a shed—
  Len'th about a half a mild!
Had about a *thousan'* head
  O' hives, I reckon—tame and wild!
Durndest buzzin' ever wuz—
Wuss'n telegraph-poles does
When they're sockin' home the news
Tight as they kin let 'er loose!
Visitors rag out and come
Clean from town to hear 'em hum,
And stop at the kivered bridge;
But wuz some 'u'd cross the ridge
Allus, and go clos'ter—so's
They could *see* 'em hum, I s'pose!
'Peared-like strangers down that track
Allus met folks comin' back
Lookin' extry fat and hearty
Fer a city picnic party!

" 'Fore he went to Floridy,
Old 'Bee' Fessler," Ike says-he—
"Old 'Bee' Fessler couldn't bide
  Childern on his place," says Ike.
"Yit, fer all, they'd climb inside
  And tromp round there, keerless-like,

In their bare feet. 'Bee' could tell
Ev'ry town-boy by his yell—
So's 'at when they bounced the fence,
Didn't make no difference!
He'd jes' git down on one knee
In the grass and pat the bee!—
And, ef 't 'adn't stayed stuck in,
Fess' 'u'd set the sting ag'in,
'N' potter off, and wait around
Fer the old famillyer sound.
Allus boys there, more or less,
Scootin' round the premises!
When the buckwheat wuz in bloom,
Lawzy! how them bees 'u'd boom
Round the boys 'at crossed that way
Fer the crick on Saturday!
Never seemed to me su'prisin'
'At the sting o' bees 'uz p'izin!

" 'Fore he went to Floridy,"
Ike says, "nothin' 'bout a bee
   'At old Fessler didn't know,—
W'y, it jes' 'peared-like 'at he
   Knowed their language, high and low
Claimed he told jes' by their buzz
What their wants and wishes wuz!

Peek in them-air little holes
    Round the porches o' the hive—
Drat their pesky little souls!—
    Could 'a' skinned the man alive!
Bore right in there with his thumb,
And squat down and scrape the gum
Outen ev'ry hole, and blow
'N' bresh the crumbs off, don't you know!
Take the roof off, and slide back
Them-air glass concerns they pack
Full o' honey, and jes' lean
'N' grabble 'mongst 'em fer the queen!
Fetch her out and *show* you to her—
Jes', you might say, *interview* her!

"Year er two," says Ike, says-he,
" 'Fore he went to Floridy,
Fessler struck the theory,
    Honey was the same as *love*—
        You could make it day and night:
Said them bees o' his could be
    Got jes' twic't the work out of
        Ef a feller managed right.
He contended ef bees found
Blossoms all the year around,
He could git 'em down at once
To work all the *winter* months

Same as *summer*. So, one fall,
  When their summer's work wuz done,
'Bee' turns in and robs 'em all;
  Loads the hives then, one by one,
On the cyars, and 'lowed he'd see
Ef bees loafed in *Floridy!*
Said he bet he'd know the reason
Ef *his* didn't work that season!

"And," says Ike, "it's jes'," says-he,
"Like old Fessler says to me:
'Any man kin fool a *bee*,
Git him down in Floridy!'
'Peared at fust, as old 'Bee' said,
Fer to kind o' turn their head
Fer a spell; but, bless you! they
Didn't lose a half a day
  Altogether!—Jes' lit in
    Them-air tropics, and them-air
  Cacktusses a-ripen-nin',
'N' magnolyers, and sweet-peas,
'N' 'simmon and pineapple trees,
    'N' ripe bananers, here and there,
'N' dates a-danglin' in the breeze,
    'N' figs and reezins ev'rywhere,
All waitin' jes' fer Fessler's bees!
'N' Fessler's bees, with gaumy wings,
A-gittin' down and *whoopin'* things!—

Fessler kind o' overseein'
'Em, and sort o' *'hee-o-heein'!*

" 'Fore he went to *Floridy*,
Old 'Bee' Fessler," Ike says-he,
"Wuzn't counted, jes' to say,
Mean er or'n'ry anyway;
On'y ev'ry 'tarnel dime
   'At 'u'd pass him on the road
He'd ketch up with, ev'ry time;
   And no mortal ever knowed
Him to spend a copper cent—
'Less on some fool-*'speriment*
With them *bees*—like that-un he
Played on 'em in Floridy.
Fess', of course, *he* tuck his ease,
But 'twuz *bilious* on the bees!
Sweat, you know, 'u'd jes' stand out
   On their *forreds*—pant and groan,
And grunt round and limp about!—
   And old 'Bee,' o' course, a-knowin'
'Twuzn't no fair shake to play
   On them pore dumb insecks, ner
To abuse 'em thataway.
Bees has rights, I'm here to say,
   And that's all they ast him fer!

Man as mean as *that*, jes' 'pears,
Could 'a' worked bees on the sheers!
Cleared big money—well, I guess,
'Bee' shipped honey, more er less,
Into ev'ry state, perhaps,
Ever putt down in the maps!

"But by time he fetched 'em back
  In the spring ag'in," says Ike,
  "They wuz actin' s'picious-like:
Though they 'peared to lost the track
  O' ev'rything they saw er heard,
    They'd lay round the porch, and gap'
At their shadders in the sun,
  Do-less like, ontel some bird
    Suddently 'u'd maybe drap
  In a bloomin' churry tree,
Twitterin' a tune 'at run
  In their minds familiously!
They'd revive up, kind o', then,
Like they argied: 'Well, it's be'n
The most longest summer we
Ever saw er want to see!
Must be *right*, though, er old "*Bee*"
'U'd notify us!' they says-ee;

And they'd sort o' square their chin
And git down to work ag'in—
Moanin' round their honey-makin',
Kind o' like their head was achin'.
Tetchin' fer to see how they
Trusted Fessler thataway—
Him a-lazin' round, and smirkin'
To hisse'f to see 'em workin'!

"But old 'Bee,' " says Ike, says-he,—
    "*Now* where is he?   *Where's* he gone?
Where's the head he helt so free?
Where's his pride and vanity?
    What's his hopes a-restin' on?—
Never knowed a man," says Ike,
    "Take advantage of a bee,
'At affliction didn't strike
    Round in that vicinity!
Sinners allus suffers some,
And *old Fessler's* reck'nin' come!
That-air man to-day is jes'
Like the grass 'at Scriptur' says
Cometh up, and then turns in
And jes' gits cut down ag'in!

Old 'Bee' Fessler," Ike says-he,
"Says, last fall, says he to me—
'Ike,' says he, 'them bees has jes'
Ciphered out my or'n'riness!
Nary bee in ary swarm
On the whole endurin' farm
Won't have nothin' more to do
   With a man as mean as I've
Be'n to them, last year er two!
   Nary bee in ary hive
But'll turn his face away,
Like they ort, whenever they
Hear my footprints drawin' nigh!'
And old 'Bee,' he'd sort o' shy
   Round oneasy in his cheer,
Wipe his eyes, and yit the sap,
Spite o' all, 'u'd haf' to drap,
   As he wound up: 'Wouldn't keer
Quite so much ef they'd jes' light
In and settle things up right,
Like they ort; but—blame the thing!—
'Pears-like they won't even *sting!*
Pepper me, the way I felt,
And I'd thank 'em, ev'ry welt!'

And as miz'able and mean
As 'Bee' looked, ef you'd 'a' seen
Them-air hungry eyes," says Ike,
"You'd fergive him, more'n like.

"Wisht you had 'a' knowed old 'Bee'
'Fore he went to Floridy!"

THE OLD TRUNDLE-BED

O THE old trundle-bed where I slept when a boy!
What canopied king might not covet the joy?
The glory and peace of that slumber of mine,
Like a long, gracious rest in the bosom divine:
The quaint, homely couch, hidden close from the light,
But daintily drawn from its hiding at night.
O a nest of delight, from the foot to the head,
Was the queer little, dear little, old trundle-bed!

O the old trundle-bed, where I wondering saw
The stars through the window, and listened with awe
To the sigh of the winds as they tremblingly crept
Through the trees where the robin so restlessly slept:
Where I heard the low, murmurous chirp of the wren,
And the katydid listlessly chirrup again,
Till my fancies grew faint and were drowsily led
Through the maze of the dreams of the old trundle-bed.

O the old trundle-bed!   O the old trundle-bed!
With its plump little pillow, and old-fashioned spread;

Its snowy-white sheets, and the blankets above,
Smoothed down and tucked round with the touches of
   love;
The voice of my mother to lull me to sleep
With the old fairy stories my memories keep
Still fresh as the lilies that bloom o'er the head
Once bowed o'er my own in the old trundle-bed.

WHERE THE CHILDREN USED TO PLAY

THE old farm-home is Mother's yet and mine,
    And filled it is with plenty and to spare,—
    But we are lonely here in life's decline,
Though fortune smiles around us everywhere:
      We look across the gold
      Of the harvests, as of old—
The corn, the fragrant clover, and the hay;
      But most we turn our gaze,
      As with eyes of other days,
To the orchard where the children used to play.

O from our life's full measure
And rich hoard of worldly treasure
  We often turn our weary eyes away,
And hand in hand we wander
Down the old path winding yonder
  To the orchard where the children used to play

Our sloping pasture-lands are filled with herds;
　　The barn and granary-bins are bulging o'er;
The grove's a paradise of singing birds—
　　The woodland brook leaps laughing by the door;
　　　　Yet lonely, lonely still,
　　　　Let us prosper as we will,
Our old hearts seem so empty everyway—
　　　　We can only through a mist
　　　　See the faces we have kissed
In the orchard where the children used to play.

　　O from our life's full measure
　　And rich hoard of worldly treasure
　　　　We often turn our weary eyes away,
　　'And hand in hand we wander
　　Down the old path winding yonder
　　　　To the orchard where the children used to play

THE HOSS

THE hoss he is a splendud beast;
   He is man's friend, as heaven desined,
   And, search the world from west to east,
No honester you'll ever find!

Some calls the hoss "a pore dumb brute,"
   And yit, like Him who died fer you,
I say, as I theyr charge refute,
   " 'Fergive; they know not what they do!' "

No wiser animal makes tracks
   Upon these earthly shores, and hence
Arose the axium, true as facts,
   Extoled by all, as "Good hoss-sense!"

The hoss is strong, and knows his stren'th,—
   You hitch him up a time er two
And lash him, and he'll go his len'th
   And kick the dashboard out fer you!

But, treat him allus good and kind,
    And never strike him with a stick,
Ner aggervate him, and you'll find
    He'll never do a hostile trick.

A hoss whose master tends him right
    And worters him with daily care,
Will do your biddin' with delight,
    And act as docile as *you* air.

He'll paw and prance to hear your praise,
    Because he's learnt to love you well;
And, though you can't tell what he says,
    He'll nicker all he wants to tell.

He knows you when you slam the gate
    At early dawn, upon your way
Unto the barn, and snorts elate,
    To git his corn, er oats, er hay.

He knows you, as the orphant knows
    The folks that loves her like theyr own,
And raises her and "finds" her clothes,
    And "schools" her tel a womern-grown!

I claim no hoss will harm a man,
   Ner kick, ner run away, cavort,
Stump-suck, er balk, er "catamaran,"
   Ef you'll jest treat him as you ort.

But when I see the beast abused,
   And clubbed around as I've saw some,
I want to see his owner noosed,
   And jest yanked up like Absolum!

Of course they's differunce in stock,—
   A hoss that has a little yeer,
And slender build, and shaller hock,
   Can beat his shadder, mighty near!

Whilse one that's thick in neck and chist
   And big in leg and full in flank,
That tries to race, I still insist
   He'll have to take the second rank.

And I have jest laid back and laughed,
   And rolled and wallered in the grass
At fairs, to see some heavy-draft
   Lead out at *first*, yit come in *last!*

Each hoss has his appinted place,—
　　The heavy hoss should plow the soil;—
The blooded racer, he must race,
　　And win big wages fer his toil.

I never bet—ner never wrought
　　Upon my feller man to bet—
And yit, at times, I've often thought
　　Of my convictions with regret.

I bless the hoss from hoof to head—
　　From head to hoof, and tale to mane!—
I bless the hoss, as I have said,
　　From head to hoof, and back again!

I love my God the first of all,
　　Then Him that perished on the cross,
And next, my wife,—and then I fall
　　Down on my knees and love the hoss.

OLD-FASHIONED ROSES

THEY ain't no style about 'em,
    And they're sort o' pale and faded,
    Yit the doorway here, without 'em,
Would be lonesomer, and shaded
    With a good 'eal blacker shadder
        Than the morning-glories makes,
    And the sunshine would look sadder
        Fer their good old-fashion' sakes.

I like 'em 'cause they kind o'
    Sort o' *make* a feller like 'em!
And I tell you, when I find a
    Bunch out whur the sun kin strike 'em,
        It allus sets me thinkin'
            O' the ones 'at used to grow
        And peek in thro' the chinkin'
            O' the cabin, don't you know!

And then I think o' mother,
   And how she ust to love 'em—
When they wuzn't any other,
   'Less she found 'em up above 'em!
     And her eyes, afore she shut 'em,
       Whispered with a smile and said
      We must pick a bunch and putt 'em
       In her hand when she wuz dead.

But, as I wuz a-sayin',
   They ain't no style about 'em
Very gaudy er displayin',
   But I wouldn't be without 'em—
     'Cause I'm happier in these posies,
       And the hollyhawks and sich,
      Than the hummin'-bird 'at noses
       In the roses of the rich.

GRIGGSBY'S STATION

PAP'S got his pattent-right, and rich as all creation;
    But where's the peace and comfort that we all
        had before?
Le's go a-visitin' back to Griggsby's Station—
    Back where we ust to be so happy and so pore!

The likes of us a-livin' here! It's jest a mortal pity
    To see us in this great big house, with cyarpets on the
        stairs,
And the pump right in the kitchen! And the city! city!
    city!—
    And nothin' but the city all around us ever'wheres!

Climb clean above the roof and look from the steeple,
    And never see a robin, nor a beech or ellum tree!
And right here in ear-shot of at least a thousan' people,
    And none that neighbors with us or we want to go and
        see!

Le's go a-visitin' back to Griggsby's Station—
   Back where the latch-string's a-hangin' from the door,
And ever' neighbor round the place is dear as a relation—
   Back where we ust to be so happy and so pore!

I want to see the Wiggenses, the whole kit-and-bilin',
   A-drivin' up from Shallor Ford to stay the Sunday through;
And I want to see 'em hitchin' at their son-in-law's and pilin'
   Out there at 'Lizy Ellen's like they ust to do!

I want to see the piece-quilts the Jones girls is makin';
   And I want to pester Laury 'bout their freckled hired hand,
And joke her 'bout the widower she come purt' nigh a-takin',
   Till her Pap got his pension 'lowed in time to save his land.

Le's go a-visitin' back to Griggsby's Station—
   Back where they's nothin' aggervatin' any more,
Shet away safe in the woods around the old location—
   Back where we ust to be so happy and so pore!

I want to see Marindy and he'p her with her sewin',
   And hear her talk so lovin' of her man that's dead and gone,
And stand up with Emanuel to show me how he's growin',
   And smile as I have saw her 'fore she putt her mournin' on.

And I want to see the Samples, on the old lower eighty,
   Where John, our oldest boy, he was tuk and burried—for
His own sake and Katy's,—and I want to cry with Katy
   As she reads all his letters over, writ from The War.

What's in all this grand life and high situation,
   And nary pink nor hollyhawk a-bloomin' at the door?—
Le's go a-visitin' back to Griggsby's Station—
   Back where we ust to be so happy and so pore!

KNEE-DEEP IN JUNE

I

TELL you what I like the best—
　'Long about knee-deep in June,
　'Bout the time strawberries melts
On the vine,—some afternoon
　Like to jes' git out and rest,
　　And not work at nothin' else!

II

Orchard's where I'd ruther be—
Needn't fence it in fer me!—
　Jes' the whole sky overhead,
And the whole airth underneath—
Sort o' so's a man kin breathe
　Like he ort, and kind o' has
Elbow-room to keerlessly
　Sprawl out len'thways on the grass
　　Where the shadders thick and soft
　As the kivvers on the bed
　　Mother fixes in the loft
Allus, when they's company!

III

Jes' a-sort o' lazin' there—
  S'lazy, 'at you peek and peer
    Through the wavin' leaves above,
    Like a feller 'at's in love
  And don't know it, ner don't keer!
  Ever'thing you hear and see
    Got some sort o' interest—
    Maybe find a bluebird's nest
  Tucked up there conveenently
  Fer the boy 'at's ap' to be
  Up some other apple-tree!
Watch the swallers skootin' past
'Bout as peert as you could ast;
  Er the Bob-white raise and whiz
  Where some other's whistle is.

IV

Ketch a shadder down below,
And look up to find the crow—
Er a hawk,—away up there,
'Pearantly *froze* in the air!—
  Hear the old hen squawk, and squat
  Over ever' chick she's got,
Suddent-like!—and she knows where

That-air hawk is, well as you!—
You jes' bet yer life she do!—
   Eyes a-glitterin' like glass,
   Waitin' till he makes a pass!

V

Pee-wees' singin', to express
   My opinion, 's second class,
Yit you'll hear 'em more er less;
   Sapsucks gittin' down to biz,
Weedin' out the lonesomeness;
   Mr. Bluejay, full o' sass,
     In them base-ball clothes o' his,
Sportin' round the orchard jes'
Like he owned the premises!
   Sun out in the fields kin sizz,
But flat on yer back, I guess,
   In the shade's where glory is!
That's jes' what I'd like to do
Stiddy fer a year er two!

VI

Plague! ef they ain't somepin' in
Work 'at kind o' goes ag'in'

My convictions!—'long about
   Here in June especially!—
    Under some old apple-tree,
       Jes' a-restin' through and through
I could git along without
       Nothin' else at all to do
       Only jes' a-wishin' you
Wuz a-gittin' there like me,
And June was eternity!

VII

Lay out there and try to see
Jes' how lazy you kin be!—
   Tumble round and souse yer head
In the clover-bloom, er pull
      Yer straw hat acrost yer eyes
      And peek through it at the skies,
  Thinkin' of old chums 'at's dead,
      Maybe, smilin' back at you
In betwixt the beautiful
      Clouds o' gold and white and blue!—
Month a man kin railly love—
June, you know, I'm talkin' of!

VIII

March ain't never nothin' new!—
Aprile's altogether too
   Brash fer me! and May—I jes'
   'Bominate its promises,—
Little hints o' sunshine and
Green around the timber-land—
   A few blossoms, and a few
   Chip-birds, and a sprout er two,—
Drap asleep, and it turns in
'Fore daylight and *snows* ag'in!—
But when *June* comes—Clear my th'oat
   With wild honey!—Rench my hair
In the dew! and hold my coat!
     Whoop out loud! and th'ow my hat!—
June wants me, and I'm to spare!
Spread them shadders anywhere,
I'll git down and waller there,
   And obleeged to you at that!

RABBIT

I S'POSE it takes a feller 'at's be'n
Raised in a country-town, like me,
To *'preciate* rabbits! . . . Eight er ten
  Bellerin' boys and two er three
Yelpin' dawgs all on the trail
O' one little pop-eyed cottontail!

'Bout the first good fall o' snow—
So's you kin track 'em, don't you know,
Where they've run,—and one by one
Hop 'em up and chase 'em down
    And prod 'em out of a' old bresh-pile
Er a holler log they're a-hidin' roun',
      Er way en-nunder the ricked cord-wood
Er crosstie-stack by the railroad track
  'Bout a mile
Out o' sight o' the whole ding town! . . .
    Well! them's times 'at I call good!

Rabbits!—w'y, as my thoughts goes back
  To them old boyhood days o' mine,
I kin sic him now and see "Old Jack"
A-plowin' snow in a rabbit-track
    And a-pitchin' over him, head and heels,
Like a blame' hat-rack,
  As the rabbit turns fer the timber-line
    Down the County Ditch through the old
        corn-fields. . . .

Yes, and I'll say right here to you,
  Rabbits that boys has *earnt*, like that—
Skinned and hung fer a night er two
    On the old back-porch where the pump's done
        froze—
Then fried 'bout right, where your brekfust's at,
With hot brown gravy and shortenin' bread,—
Rabbits, like *them*—er I ort to 'a' said,
    I s'pose,
    Rabbits like *those*
Ain't so p'ticalar pore, I guess,
Fer *eatin'* purposes!

SYMPTOMS

I 'M not a-workin' now!—
   I'm jes' a-layin' round
   A-lettin' *other* people plow.—
I'm cumberin' the ground! . . .
I jes' don't *keer!*—I've done my sheer
   O' sweatin'!—Anyhow,
In this dad-blasted weather here,
   I'm not a-workin' *now!*

The corn and wheat and all
   Is doin' well enough!—
They' got clean on from now tel Fall
   To show what kind o' stuff
'At's in their *own* dad-burn backbone;
   So, while the Scriptur's 'low
Man ort to reap as he have sown—
   I'm not a-workin' now!

The grass en-nunder these-
  Here ellums 'long "Old Blue,"
And shadders o' the sugar-trees,
  Beats farmin' quite a few!
As feller says,—I ruther guess
  I'll make my comp'ny bow
And *snooze* a few hours—more er less.—
  I'm not a-workin' now!

HIS PA'S ROMANCE

ALL 'at I ever want to be
   Is ist to be a man like Pa
   When he wuz young an' married Ma!
Uncle he telled us yisterdy
Ist all about it then—'cause they,
My Pa an' Ma, wuz bofe away
To 'tend P'tracted Meetin', where
My Pa an' Ma is allus there
When all the big "Revivals" is,
An' "Love-Feasts," too, an' "Class," an' "Prayer,"
An' when's "Comoonian Servicis."
An', yes, an' Uncle said to not
To never tell *them* nor let on
Like we knowed now ist how they got
First married. So—while they wuz gone—
Uncle he telled us ever'thing—
'Bout how my Paw wuz ist a pore
Farm-boy.—He says, I tell you *what*,

Your Pa *wuz* pore! But neighbors they
All liked him—all but one old man
An' his old wife that folks all say
Nobody liked, ner never can!

Yes, sir! an' Uncle purt' nigh swore
About the mean old man an' way
He treat' my Pa!—'cause he's a pore
Farm-hand—but prouder 'an a king—
An' ist work' on, he did, an' wore
His old patched clo'es, ist anyway,
So he saved up his wages—then
He ist worked on an' saved some more,
An' ist worked on, ist night an' day—
Till, sir, he save' up nine or ten
Er hunnerd dollars! But he keep
All still about it, Uncle say—
But he ist thinks—an' thinks a heap!
Though what he wuz a-thinkin', Pa
He never tell' a soul but Ma—
(Then, course, you know, he wuzn't Pa,
An', course, you know, she wuzn't Ma—
They wuz ist sweethearts, course you know);
'Cause Ma wuz ist a girl, about
Sixteen; an' when my Pa he go
A-courtin' her, her Pa an' Ma—
The very first they find it out—

Wuz maddest folks you ever saw!
'Cause it wuz her old Ma an' Pa
'At hate my Pa, an' toss their head,
An' ist raise Ned! An' her Pa said
He'd ruther see his daughter dead!
An' said she's ist a child!—an' so
Wuz Pa!—An' ef he wuz man-grown
An' only man on earth below,
His daughter shouldn't marry him
Ef he's a king an' on his throne!
Pa's chances then looked mighty slim
Fer certain, Uncle said. But he—
He never told a soul but her
What he wuz keepin' quiet fer.
Her folks ist lived a mile from where
He lived at—an' they drove past there
To git to town. An' ever' one
An' all the neighbers they liked her
An' showed it! But her folks—no, sir!—
Nobody liked her parunts none!
An' so when they shet down, you know,
On Pa—an' old man tell' him so—
Pa ist went back to work, an' she
Ist waited. An', sir! purty soon
Her folks they thought he's turned his eye
Some other way—'cause by-an'-by

They heard he'd *rented* the old place
He worked on. An' one afternoon
A neighber, that had bu'st' a trace,
He tell' the old man they wuz signs
Around the old place that the young
Man wuz a-fixin' up the old
Log cabin some, an' he had brung
New furnichur from town; an' told
How th' old house 'uz whitewashed clean
An' sweet—wiv mornin'-glory vines
An' hollyhawks all 'round the door
An' winders—an' a bran'-new floor
In th' old porch—an' wite-new green-
An'-red pump in the old sweep-well!
An', Uncle said, when he hear tell
O' all them things, the old man he
Ist grin' an' says, he "reckon' now
Some gal, er widder anyhow,
That silly boy he's coaxed at last
To marry him!" he says, says-ee,
"An' ef he has, 'so mote it be'!"
Then went back to the house to tell
His *wife* the news, as he went past
The smokehouse, an' then went on in
The kitchen, where his daughter she
Wuz washin', to tell *her*, an' grin
An' try to worry her a spell!

The mean old thing! But Uncle said
She ain't cry much—ist pull her old
Sunbonnet forrerds on her head—
So's old man he can't see her face
At all! An' when he s'pose he scold'
An' jaw enough, he ist clear' out
An' think he's boss of all the place!

Then Uncle say, the first you know
They's go' to be a Circus-show
In town! an' old man think he'll take
His wife an' go. An' when she say
To take their daughter, too, *she* shake
Her head like she don't *want* to go;
An' when he sees she wants to stay,
The old man takes her, anyway!
An' so she went! But Uncle he
Said she looked mighty sweet that day,
Though she wuz pale as she could be,
A-speshully a-drivin' by
Wite where her beau lived at, you know;
But out the corner of his eye
The old man watch' her; but she throw
Her pairsol 'round so she can't see
The house at all! An' then she hear
Her Pa an' Ma a-talkin' low
And kind o' laughin'-like; but she

Ist set there in the seat behind,
P'tendin' like she didn't mind.
An', Uncle say, when they got past
The young man's place, an' 'pearantly
He wuzn't home, but off an' gone
To town, the old man turned at last
An' talked back to his daughter there,
All pleasant-like, from then clean on
Till they got into town, an' where
The Circus wuz, an' on inside
O' that, an' through the crowd, on to
The very top seat in the tent
Wite next the band—a-bangin' through
A tune 'at bu'st his yeers in two!
An' there the old man scrouged an' tried
To make his wife set down, an' she
A-yellin'! But ist what she meant
He couldn't hear, ner couldn't see
Till she turned 'round an' pinted. Then
He turned an' looked—an' looked again!
He ist saw neighbers ever'where—
But, sir, *his daughter* wuzn't there!
An', Uncle says, he even saw
Her beau, you know, he hated so;
An' he wuz with some other girl.
An' then he heard the Clown "Haw-haw!"

An' saw the horses wheel an' whin'
Around the ring, an' heard the zipp
O' the Ringmaster's long slim whip—
But that whole Circus, Uncle said,
Wuz all inside the old man's head!

An' Uncle said, he didn't find
His daughter all that afternoon—
An' her Ma says she'll lose her mind
Ef they don't find her purty soon!
But, though they looked all day, an' stayed
There fer the night p'formance—not
No use at all!—they never laid
Their eyes on her. An' then they got
Their team out, an' the old man shook
His fist at all the town, an' then
Shook it up at the moon ag'in,
An' said his time 'ud come, some day!
An' jerked the lines an' driv away.

Uncle, he said, he 'spect, that night,
The old man's madder yet when they
Drive past the young man's place, an' hear
A fiddle there, an' see a light
Inside, an' shadders light an' gay

A-dancin' 'crost the winder-blinds.
An' some young chaps outside yelled, "Say!
What 'pears to be the hurry—hey?"
But the old man ist whipped the lines
An' streaked past like a runaway!
An' now you'll be su'prised, I bet!—
I hardly ain't quit laughin' yet
When Uncle say, that jamboree
An' dance an' all—w'y, that's a sign
That any old man ort to see,
As plain as 8 and 1 makes 9,
That they's *a weddin'* wite inside
That very house he's whippin' so
To git apast—an', sir! the bride
There's his own daughter! Yes, an' oh!
She's my Ma now—an' young man she
Got married, he's my Pa! *Whoop-ee!*
But Uncle say to not laugh all
The laughin' yet, but please save some
To kind o' spice up what's to come!

Then Uncle say, about next day
The neighbors they begin to call
An' wish 'em well, an' say how glad
An' proud an' tickled ever' way
Their friends all is—an' how they had

The lovin' prayers of ever' one
That had homes of their own! But none
Said nothin' 'bout the home that she
Had run away from! So she sighed
Sometimes—an' wunst she purt' nigh cried

Well, Uncle say, her old Pa, he
Ist like to died, he wuz so mad!
An' her Ma, too! But by-an'-by
They cool down some.
     An' 'bout a week,
She want to see her Ma so bad,
She think she'll haf to go! An' so
She coax him; an' he kiss her cheek
An' say, Lord bless her, *course* they'll go!
An', Uncle say, when they're bofe come
A-knockin' there at her old home—
W'y, first he know, the door it flew
Open, all quick, an' she's jerked in,
An', quicker still, the door's banged to
An' locked: an' crosst the winder-sill
The old man pokes a shotgun through
An' says to git! "You stold my child,"
He says; "an', now she's back, w'y, you
Clear out, this minute, er I'll kill
You! Yes, an' I 'ull kill her, too,
Ef you don't go!" An' then, all wild,

His young wife begs him please to go!
An' so he turn' an' walk'—all slow
An' pale as death, but awful still
An' ca'm—back to the gate, an' on
Into the road, where he had gone
So many times alone, you know!
An', Uncle say, a whipperwill
Holler so lonesome, as he go
On back to'rds home, he say he 'spec'
He ist 'ud like to wring its neck!
An' I ain't think he's goin' back
All by hisse'f—but Uncle say
That's what he does, an' it's a fac'!

An' 'pears-like he's gone back to *stay*—
'Cause there he stick', ist thataway,
An' don't go nowheres any more,
Ner don't nobody ever see
Him set his foot outside the door—
Till 'bout five days, a boy loped down
The road, a-comin' past from town,
An' he called to him from the gate,
An' sent the old man word: He's thought
Things over now; an', while he hate
To lose his wife, he think she ought
To mind her Pa an' Ma an' do
Whatever *they* advise her to.

An' sends words, too, to come an' git
Her new things an' the furnichur
That he had special' bought fer her—
'Cause, now that they wuz goin' to quit,
She's free to ist have all of it;—
So, fer his love fer her, he say
To come an' git it, wite away.
An' spang! that very afternoon,
Here come her Ma—ist 'bout as soon
As old man could hitch up an 'tell
Her "hurry back!" An' 'bout as quick
As she's drove there to where my Pa—
I mean to where her son-in-law—
Lives at, he meets her at the door
All smilin', though he's awful pale
An' trimbly—like he's ist been sick;
He take her in the house—An', 'fore
She knows it, they's a cellar-door
Shet on her, an' she hears the click
Of a' old rusty padlock! Then,
Uncle, he say, she kind o' stands
An' thinks—an' thinks—an' thinks ag'in—
An' mayby thinks of her own child
Locked up—like her! An' Uncle smiled,
An' I ist laughed an' clapped my hands!

An' there she stayed! An' she can cry
Ist all she want! an' yell an' kick
To ist her heart's content! an' try
To pry out wiv a quiltin'-stick!
But Uncle say he guess at last
She 'bout give up, an' holler' through
The door-crack fer to please to be
So kind an' good as send an' tell
The old man, like she want him to,
To come, 'fore night, an' set her free,
Er—they wuz rats down there! An' yell
She did, till, Uncle say, it soured
The morning's milk in the back yard!
But all the answer reached her, where
She's skeered so in the dark down there,
Wuz ist a mutterin' that she heard—
"*I've sent him word!—I've sent him word!*"
An' shore enough, as Uncle say,
He *has* "sent word!"

                Well, it's plum night
An' all the house is shet up tight—
Only one winder 'bout half-way
Raised up, you know; an' ain't no light
Inside the whole house, Uncle say.

Then, first you know, there where the team
Stands hitched yet, there the old man stands—
A' old tin lantern in his hands
An' monkey-wrench; an' he don't seem
To make things out, a-standin' there.
He comes on to the gate an' feels
An' fumbles fer the latch—then hears
A voice that chills him to the heels—
"You halt! an' stand right where you air!"
Then, sir! my—my—his son-in-law,
There at the winder wiv his gun,
He tell the old man what he's done:
"You hold *my* wife a prisoner—
An' *your* wife, drat ye! I've got *her!*
An' now, sir," Uncle say he say,
"You ist turn round an' climb wite in
That wagon, an' drive home ag'in
An' bring my wife back wite away,
An' we'll trade then—an' not before
Will I unlock my cellar-door—
Not fer your wife's sake ner your own,
But *my* wife's sake—an' hers alone!"
An', Uncle say, it don't sound like
It's so, but yet it is!—He say,
From wite then, somepin' seem' to strike
The old man's funny-bone some way;

An', minute more, that team o' his
Went tearin' down the road *k'whiz!*
An' in the same two-forty style
Come whizzin' back! An' oh, that-air
Sweet girl a-cryin' all the while,
Thinkin' about her Ma there, shet
In her own daughter's cellar, where
Ist week or so *she's* kep' house there,
She hadn't time to clean it yet!
So when her Pa an' her they git
There—an' the young man grab' an' kiss
An' hug her, till she make him quit
An' ask him where her mother is.
An' then he smile' an' try to not;
Then slow-like find th' old padlock key,
An' blow a' oat-hull out of it,
An' then stoop down there where he's got
Her Ma locked up so keerfully—
An' where, wite there, he say he thought
It *ort* to been *the old man*—though
Uncle, he say, he reckon not—
When out she bounced, all tickled so
To taste fresh air ag'in an' find
Her folks wunst more, an' grab' her child
An' cry an' laugh, an' even go

An' hug the old man; an' he wind
Her in his arms, an' laugh, an' pat
Her back, an' say he's riconciled,
In such a happy scene as that,
To swap his daughter for her Ma,
An' have so smart a son-in-law
As *they* had! "Yes, an' he's my Pa!"
I laugh' an' yell', "Hooray-hooraw!"

THE RAMBO-TREE

WHEN Autumn shakes the rambo-tree—
    It's a long, sweet way across the orchard!—
The bird sings low as the bumble bee—
    It's a long, sweet way across the orchard!—
The poor shote-pig he says, says he:
"When Autumn shakes the rambo-tree
There's enough for you and enough for me."—
    It's a long, sweet way across the orchard.

For just two truant lads like we,
When Autumn shakes the rambo-tree
There's enough for you and enough for me—
    It's a long, sweet way across the orchard.

When Autumn shakes the rambo-tree—
    It's a long, sweet way across the orchard!—
The mole digs out to peep and see—
    It's a long, sweet way across the orchard!—

The dusk sags down, and the moon swings free,
There's a far, lorn call, "Pig-*gee!* Pig-*gee!*"
And two boys—glad enough for three.—
   It's a long, sweet way across the orchard.

For just two truant lads like we,
When Autumn shakes the rambo-tree
There's enough for you and enough for me—
   It's a long, sweet way across the orchard.

THOUGHTS FER THE DISCURAGED FARMER

THE summer winds is sniffin' round the bloomin' locus' trees;
    And the clover in the pastur is a big day fer the bees,
And they been a-swiggin' honey, above board and on the sly,
Tel they stutter in theyr buzzin' and stagger as they fly.
The flicker on the fence-rail 'pears to jest spit on his wings
And roll up his feathers, by the sassy way he sings;
And the hoss-fly is a-whettin'-up his forelegs fer biz,
And the off-mare is a-switchin' all of her tale they is.

You can hear the blackbirds jawin' as they foller up the plow—
Oh, theyr bound to git theyr brekfast, and theyr not a-carin' how;
So they quarrel in the furries, and they quarrel on the wing—
But theyr peaceabler in pot-pies than any other thing:

And it's when I git my shotgun drawed up in stiddy rest,
She's as full of tribbelation as a yeller-jacket's nest;
And a few shots before dinner, when the sun's a-shinin'
    right,
Seems to kindo'-sorto' sharpen up a feller's appetite!

They's been a heap o' rain, but the sun's out to-day,
And the clouds of the wet spell is all cleared away,
And the woods is all the greener, and the grass is greener
    still;
It may rain again to-morry, but I don't think it will.
Some says the crops is ruined, and the corn's drownded
    out,
And propha-sy the wheat will be a failure, without
    doubt;
But the kind Providence that has never failed us yet,
Will be on hands onc't more at the 'leventh hour, I bet!

Does the medder-lark complane, as he swims high and
    dry
Through the waves of the wind and the blue of the sky?
Does the quail set up and whissel in a disappinted way,
Er hang his head in silunce, and sorrow all the day?

Is the chipmuck's health a-failin'?—Does he walk, er does he run?
Don't the buzzards ooze around up thare jest like they've allus done?
Is they anything the matter with the rooster's lungs er voice?
Ort a mortul be complanin' when dumb animals rejoice?

Then let us, one and all, be contentud with our lot;
The June is here this mornin', and the sun is shining hot.
Oh! let us fill our harts up with the glory of the day,
And banish ev'ry doubt and care and sorrow fur away!
Whatever be our station, with Providence fer guide,
Sich fine circumstances ort to make us satisfied;
Fer the world is full of roses, and the roses full of dew,
And the dew is full of heavenly love that drips fer me and you.

A SUMMER'S DAY

THE SUMMER'S put the idy in
    My head that I'm a boy ag'in;
    And all around's so bright and gay
I want to put my team away,
And jest git out whare I can lay
And soak my hide full of the day!
But work is work, and must be done—
Yit, as I work, I have my fun,
Jest fancyin' these furries here
Is childhood's paths onc't more so dear:—
And so I walk through medder-lands,
    And country lanes, and swampy trails
Whare long bullrushes bresh my hands;
    And, tilted on the ridered rails
Of deadnin' fences, "Old Bob White"
Whissels his name in high delight,
And whirrs away. I wunder still,
Whichever way a boy's feet will—

Whare trees has fell, with tangled tops
  Whare dead leaves shakes, I stop fer breth,
Heerin' the acorn as it drops—
  H'istin' my chin up still as deth,
And watchin' clos't, with upturned eyes,
The tree where Mr. Squirrel tries
To hide hisse'f above the limb,
But lets his own tale tell on him.
I wunder on in deeper glooms—
  Git hungry, hearin' female cries
From old farm-houses, whare perfumes
  Of harvest dinners seems to rise
And ta'nt a feller, hart and brane,
With memories he can't explane.

I wunder through the underbresh,
  Whare pig-tracks, pintin' to'rds the crick,
Is picked and printed in the fresh
  Black bottom-lands, like wimmern pick
Theyr pie-crusts with a fork, some way,
When bakin' fer camp-meetin' day.
I wunder on and on and on,
Tel my gray hair and beard is gone,
And ev'ry wrinkle on my brow
Is rubbed clean out and shaddered now
With curls as brown and fare and fine
As tenderls of the wild grape-vine

That ust to climb the highest tree
To keep the ripest ones fer me.
I wunder still, and here I am
Wadin' the ford below the dam—
The worter chucklin' round my knee
   At hornet-welt and bramble-scratch,
And me a-slippin' 'crost to see
      Ef Tyner's plums is ripe, and size
   The old man's wortermelon-patch,
    With juicy mouth and drouthy eyes.
Then, after sich a day of mirth
And happiness as worlds is wurth—
   So tired that Heaven seems nigh about,—
The sweetest tiredness on earth
   Is to git home and flatten out—
So tired you can't lay flat enugh,
And sorto' wish that you could spred
Out like molasses on the bed,
And jest drip off the aidges in
The dreams that never comes ag'in.

A TALE OF THE AIRLY DAYS

OH! TELL me a tale of the airly days—
    Of the times as they used to be;
  "Piller of Fi-er" and "Shakespeare's Plays"
Is a' most too deep fer me!
I want plane facts, and I want plane words,
    Of the good old-fashioned ways,
When speech run free as the songs of birds
    'Way back in the airly days.

Tell me a tale of the timber-lands—
    Of the old-time pioneers;
Somepin' a pore man understands
    With his feelin's 's well as ears.
Tell of the old log house,—about
    The loft, and the puncheon flore—
The old fi-er-place, with the crane swung out,
    And the latch-string thrugh the door.

Tell of the things jest as they was—
    They don't need no excuse!—
Don't tetch 'em up like the poets does,
    Tel theyr all too fine fer use!—
Say they was 'leven in the fambily—
    Two beds, and the chist, below,
And the trundle-beds that each helt three,
    And the clock and the old bureau.

Then blow the horn at the old back-door
    Tel the echoes all halloo,
And the childern gethers home onc't more,
    Jest as they ust to do:
Blow fer Pap tel he hears and comes,
    With Tomps and Elias, too,
A-marchin' home, with the fife and drums
    And the old Red White and Blue!

Blow and blow tel the sound draps low
    As the moan of the whipperwill,
And wake up Mother, and Ruth and Jo,
    All sleepin' at Bethel Hill:
Blow and call tel the faces all
    Shine out in the back-log's blaze,
And the shadders dance on the old hewed wall
    As they did in the airly days.

UP AND DOWN OLD BRANDYWINE

UP AND DOWN old Brandywine,
  In the days 'at's past and gone—
With a dad-burn hook-and-line
And a saplin'-pole—i swawn!
    I've had more fun, to the square
    Inch, than ever *any*where!
    Heaven to come can't discount *mine*,
    Up and down old Brandywine!

Hain't no sense in *wishin'* yit
  Wisht to goodness I *could* jes'
"Gee" the blame' world round and git
  Back to that old happiness!—
    Kind o' drive back in the shade
    "The old Covered Bridge" there laid
    'Crosst the crick, and sort o' soak
    My soul over, hub and spoke!

Honest, now!—it hain't no *dream*
    'At I'm wantin',—but *the fac's*
As they wuz; the same old stream,
    And the same old times, i jacks!—
        Gimme back my bare feet—and
        Stonebruise too!—And scratched and
            tanned!—
        And let hottest dog-days shine
        Up and down old Brandywine!

In and on betwixt the trees
    'Long the banks, pour down yer noon,
Kind o' curdled with the breeze
    And the yallerhammer's tune;
        And the smokin', chokin' dust
        O' the turnpike at its wusst—
        Saturd'ys, say, when it seems
        Road's jes' jammed with country teams!—

Whilse the old town, fur away
    'Crosst the hazy pastur'-land,
Dozed-like in the heat o' day
    Peaceful' as a hired hand.
        Jolt the gravel th'ough the floor
        O' the old bridge!—grind and roar
        With yer blame' percession-line—
        Up and down old Brandywine!

Souse me and my new straw-hat
    Off the foot-log!—what *I* care?—
Fist shoved in the crown o' that—
    Like the old Clown ust to wear.—
        Wouldn't swop it fer a' old
        Gin-u-wine raal crown o' gold!—
        Keep yer *King* ef you'll gimme
        Jes' the boy I ust to be!

Spill my fishin'-worms! er steal
    My best "goggle-eye!"—but you
Can't lay hands on joys I feel
    Nibblin' like they ust to do!
        So, in memory, to-day
        Same old ripple lips away
        At my cork and saggin' line,
        Up and down old Brandywine!

There the logs is, round the hill,
    Where "Old Irvin" ust to lift
Out sunfish from daylight till
    Dewfall—'fore he'd leave "The Drift"
        And give *us* a chance—and then
        Kind o' fish back home again,
        Ketchin' 'em jes' left and right
        Where *we* hadn't got "a bite"!

Er, 'way windin' out and in,—
    Old path th'ough the iurnweeds
And dog-fennel to yer chin—
    Then come suddent, th'ough the reeds
        And cattails, smack into where
        Them-air woods-hogs ust to scare
        Us clean 'crosst the County-line,
        Up and down old Brandywine!

But the dim roar o' the dam
    It 'ud coax us furder still
To'rds the old race, slow and ca'm,
    Slidin' on to Huston's mill—
        Where, I 'spect, "the Freeport crowd"
        Never *warmed* to us er 'lowed
        We wuz quite so overly
        Welcome as we aimed to be.

Still it 'peared-like ever'thing—
    Fur away from home as *there*—
Had more *relish*-like, i jing!—
    Fish in stream, er bird in air!
        O them rich old bottom-lands,
        Past where Cowden's Schoolhouse stands!
        Wortermelons—*master-mine!*
        Up and down old Brandywine!

And sich pop-paws!—Lumps o' raw
    Gold and green,—jes' oozy th'ough
With ripe yaller—like you've saw
    Custard-pie with no crust to:
        And jes' *gorges* o' wild plums,
        Till a feller'd suck his thumbs
        Clean up to his elbows! *My!*—
        Me some more er lem me die!

Up and down old Brandywine!
    Stripe me with pokeberry-juice!—
Flick me with a pizen-vine
    And yell "*Yip!*" and lem me loose!
        —Old now as I then wuz young,
        'F I could sing as I *have* sung,
        Song 'ud surely ring *dee-vine*
        Up and down old Brandywine!

UNCLE DAN'L IN TOWN OVER SUNDAY.

I CAIN'T git used to city ways—
  Ner ever could, I' bet my hat!
  Jevver know jes' whur I was raised?—
Raised on a farm! D' ever tell you that?
Was undoubtatly, I declare!
And now, on Sunday—fun to spare
Around a farm! Why jes' to set
Up on the top three-cornered rail
Of Pap's old place, nigh La Fayette,
I'd swap my soul off, hide and tail!
You fellers in the city here,
You don't know nothin'!—S'pose to-day,
This clatterin' Sunday, you waked up
Without no jinglin'-janglin' bells,
Ner rattlin' of the milkman's cup,
Ner any swarm of screechin' birds
Like these here English swallers—S'pose
Ut you could miss all noise like those,
And git shet o' thinkin' of 'em afterwerds,

And then, in the country, wake and hear
Nothin' but silence—wake and see
Nothin' but green woods fur and near?—
What sort o' Sunday would that be? . .
Wisht I hed you home with me!
Now think! The laziest of all days—
To git up any time—er sleep—
Er jes' lay round and watch the haze
A-dancin' 'crost the wheat, and keep
My pipe a-goern laisurely,
And puff and whiff as pleases me—
And ef I leave a trail of smoke
Clean through the house, no one to say,
"Wah! throw that nasty thing away;
Hev some regyard fer decency!"
To walk round barefoot, if you choose;
Er saw the fiddle—er dig some bait
And go a-fishin'—er pitch hoss shoes
Out in the shade somewhurs, and wait
For dinner-time, with an appetite
Ut folks in town cain't equal quite!
To laze around the barn and poke
Fer hens' nests—er git up a match
Betwixt the boys, and watch 'em scratch

And rassle round, and sweat and swear
And quarrel to their hearts' content;
And me a-jes' a-settin' there
A-hatchin' out more devilment!
What sort o' Sunday would that be? . . .
Wisht I hed you home with me!

WHEN THE GREEN GITS BACK IN THE TREES

IN SPRING, when the green gits back in the trees,
    And the sun comes out and *stays*,
  And yer boots pulls on with a good tight squeeze,
    And you think of yer barefoot days;
When you *ort* to work and you want to *not*,
    And you and yer wife agrees
It's time to spade up the garden-lot,
    When the green gits back in the trees—
      Well! work is the least o' *my* idees
      When the green, you know, gits back in the trees!

When the green gits back in the trees, and bees
    Is a-buzzin' aroun' ag'in,
In that kind of a lazy go-as-you-please
    Old gait they bum roun' in;
When the groun's all bald where the hay-rick stood,
    And the crick's riz, and the breeze
Coaxes the bloom in the old dogwood,
    And the green gits back in the trees,—

I like, as I say, in sich scenes as these,
The time when the green gits back in the trees!

When the whole tail-feathers o' Winter-time
   Is all pulled out and gone!
And the sap it thaws and begins to climb,
   And the swet it starts out on
A feller's forred, a-gittin' down
   At the old spring on his knees—
I kindo' like jest a-loaferin' roun'
   When the green gits back in the trees—
      Jest a-potterin' roun' as I—durn—please—
      When the green, you know, gits back in the trees!

DOC SIFERS

OF ALL the doctors I could cite you to in this-
    'ere town
  Doc Sifers is my favorite, jes' take him up and
    down!
Count in the Bethel Neighborhood, and Rollins, and Big
    Bear,
And Sifers' standin's jes' as good as ary doctor's there!

There's old Doc Wick, and Glenn, and Hall, and
    Wurgler, and McVeigh,
But I'll buck Sifers 'g'inst 'em all and down 'em any
    day!
Most old Wick ever knowed, I s'pose, was *whisky!*
    Wurgler—well,
He et morphine—ef actions shows, and facts' reliable!

But Sifers—though he ain't no sot, he's got his faults;
    and yit
When you *git* Sifers onc't, you've got *a doctor*, don't
    fergit!

He ain't much at his office, er his house, er anywhere
You'd natchurly think certain fer to ketch the feller there.—

But don't blame Doc: he's got all sorts o' cur'ous notions—as
The feller says, his odd-come-shorts, like smart men mostly has.
He'll more'n like be potter'n' 'round the Blacksmith Shop; er in
Some back lot, spadin' up the ground, er gradin' it ag'in.

Er at the work bench, planin' things; er buildin' little traps
To ketch birds; galvenizin' rings; er graftin' plums, perhaps.
Make anything! good as the best!—a gun-stock—er a flute;
He whittled out a set o' chesstmen onc't o' laurel root,

Durin' the Army—got his trade o' surgeon there—I own
To-day a finger-ring Doc made out of a Sesesh bone!
An' glued a fiddle onc't fer me—jes' all so busted you
'D 'a' throwed the thing away, but he fixed her as good as new!

And take Doc, now, in *ager*, say, er *biles*, er *rheumatiz*,
And all afflictions thataway, and he's the best they is!
Er janders—milksick—I don't keer—k-yore anything he tries—
A abscess; getherin' in yer yeer; er granilated eyes!

There was the Widder Daubenspeck they all give up fer dead;
A blame cowbuncle on her neck, and clean out of her head!
First had this doctor, what's-his-name, from "Puddlesburg," and then
This little red-head, "Burnin' Shame" they call him— Dr. Glenn.

And they "consulted" on the case, and claimed she'd haf to die, —
I jes' was joggin' by the place, and heerd her dorter cry,
And stops and calls her to the fence; and I-says-I, "Let me
Send Sifers—bet you fifteen cents he'll k-yore her!" "Well," says she,

"Light out!" she says: And, lipp-tee-cut I loped in town, and rid
'Bout two hours more to find him, but I kussed him when I did!

156

He was down at the Gunsmith Shop a-stuffin' birds!
   Says he,
"My sulky's broke." Says I, "You hop right on and ride
   with me!"

I got him there.—"Well, Aunty, ten days k-yores you,"
   Sifers said,
"But what's yer idy livin' when yer jes' as good as
   dead?"
And there's Dave Banks—jes' back from war without a
   scratch—one day
Got ketched up in a sickle-bar, a reaper runaway.—

His shoulders, arms, and hands and legs jes' sawed in
   strips!   And Jake
Dunn starts fer Sifers—feller begs to shoot him fer God-
   sake.
Doc, 'course, was gone, but he had penned the notice,
   "At Big Bear—
Be back to-morry; Gone to 'tend the Bee Convention
   there."

But Jake, he tracked him—rid and rode the whole en-
   durin' night!
And 'bout the time the roosters crowed they both hove
   into sight.

Doc had to ampitate, but 'greed to save Dave's arms, and swore
He could 'a' saved his legs ef he'd b'en there the day before.

Like when his wife's own mother died 'fore Sifers could be found,
And all the neighbers fer and wide a' all jes' chasin' round;
Tel finally—I had to laugh—it's jes' like Doc, you know,—
Was learnin' fer to telegraph, down at the old deepo.

But all they're faultin' Sifers fer, there's none of 'em kin say
He's biggoty, er keerless, er not posted anyway;
He ain't built on the common plan of doctors now-a-days,
He's jes' a great, big, brainy man—that's where the trouble lays!

DOWN AROUND THE RIVER

NOON-TIME and June-time, down around the
    river!
    Have to furse with Lizey Ann—but lawzy! I
fergive her!
Drives me off the place, and says 'at all 'at she's a-
    wishin',
Land o' gracious! time'll come I'll git enough o' fishin'!
Little Dave, a-choppin' wood, never 'pears to notice;
Don't know where she's hid his hat, er keerin' where
    his coat is,—
Specalatin', more'n like, he hain't a-goin' to mind me,
And guessin' where, say twelve o'clock, a feller'd likely
    find me.

Noon-time and June-time, down around the river!
Clean out o' sight o' home, and skulkin' under kivver
Of the sycamores, jack-oaks, and swamp-ash and el-
    lum—
Idies all so jumbled up you kin hardly tell 'em!—

Tired, you know, but *lovin'* it, and smilin' jes' to think
  'at
Any sweeter tiredness you'd fairly want to *drink* it.
Tired o' fishin'—tired o' fun—line out slack and
  slacker—
All you want in all the world's a little more tobacker!

Hungry, but *a-hidin'* it, er jes' a-not a-kerrin':—
Kingfisher gittin' up and skootin' out o' hearin';
Snipes on the t'other side, where the County Ditch is,
Wadin' up and down the aidge like they'd rolled their
  britches!
Old turkle on the root kind o' sort o' drappin'
Intoo th' worter like he don't know how it happen!
Worter, shade and all so mixed, don't know which you'd
  orter
Say, th' *worter* in the shadder—*shadder* in the *worter*.

Somebody hollerin'—'way around the bend in
Upper Fork—where yer eye kin jes' ketch the endin'
Of the shiney wedge o' wake some muss-rat's a-makin'
With that pesky nose o' his! Then a sniff o' bacon,
Corn-bread and 'dock-greens—and little Dave a-shinnin'
'Crost the rocks and mussel-shells, a-limpin' and a-
  grinnin',
With yer dinner fer ye, and a blessin' from the giver.
Noon-time and June-time down around the river!

HIS ROOM

I'M home again, my dear old Room,
   I'm home again, and happy, too,
As, peering through the brightening gloom,
I find myself alone with you:
   Though brief my stay, nor far away,
   I missed you—missed you night and day—
   As wildly yearned for you as now.—
   Old Room, how are you, anyhow?

My easy chair, with open arms,
   Awaits me just within the door;
The littered carpet's woven charms
   Have never seemed so bright before,—
   The old rosettes and mignonettes
   And ivy-leaves and violets,
   Look up as pure and fresh of hue
   As though baptized in morning-dew.

Old Room, to me your homely walls
   Fold round me like the arms of love,
And over all my being falls
   A blessing pure as from above—

Even as a nestling child caressed
And lulled upon a loving breast,
With folded eyes, too glad to weep
And yet too sad for dreams or sleep.

You've been so kind to me, old Room—
　So patient in your tender care,
My drooping heart in fullest bloom
　Has blossomed for you unaware;
　　And who but you had cared to woo
　　A heart so dark, and heavy too,
　　As in the past you lifted mine
　　From out the shadow to the shine?

For I was but a wayward boy
　When first you gladly welcomed me
And taught me work was truer joy
　Than rioting incessantly:
　　And thus the din that stormed within
　　The old guitar and violin
　　Has fallen in a fainter tone
　　And sweeter, for your sake alone.

Though in my absence I have stood
　In festal halls a favored guest,
I missed, in this old quietude,
　My worthy work and worthy rest—

162

By *this* I know that long ago
You loved me first, and told me so
In art's mute eloquence of speech
The voice of praise may never reach.

For lips and eyes in truth's disguise
  Confuse the faces of my friends,
Till old affection's fondest ties
  I find unraveling at the ends;
    But, as I turn to you, and learn
    To meet my griefs with less concern,
    Your love seems all I have to keep
    Me smiling lest I needs must weep.

Yet I am happy, and would fain
  Forget the world and all its woes;
So set me to my tasks again,
  Old Room, and lull me to repose:
    And as we glide adown the tide
    Of dreams, forever side by side,
    I'll hold your hands as lovers do
    Their sweethearts' and talk love to you

CUORED O' SKEERIN'

'LISH, you rickollect that-air
    Dad-burn skittish old bay mare
      Was no livin' with!—'at skeerd
'T ever'thing she seed er heerd!—
Th'owed 'Ves' Anders, and th'owed Pap,
First he straddled her—*k-slap!*—
And Izory—well!—th'owed *her*
Hain't no tellin' jest how fur!—
Broke her collar-bone—and **might**
Jest 'a' kilt the gyrl outright!

Course I'd heerd 'em make their boast
She th'ow any feller, 'most,
Ever topped her! S' I, "I know
One man 'at she'll never th'ow!"
So I rid her into mill,
And, jest comin' round the hill,
Met a *traction-engine!*—Ort
Jest 'a' heerd that old mare snort,
And lay back her yeers, and see
Her a-tryin' to th'ow *me!*

Course I never said a word,
But thinks I, "My ladybird,
You'll git cuored, right here and now,
Of yer dy-does anyhow!"
So I stuck her—tel she'd jest
Done her very level best;
Then I slides off—strips the lines
Over her fool-head, and finds
Me a little saplin'-gad,
'Side the road:—And there we had
Our own fun!—jest wore her out!
Mounted her, and faced about,
And jest made her *nose* that-air
Little traction-engine there!

FARMER WHIPPLE.—BACHELOR

IT'S a mystery to see me—a man o' fifty-four,
  Who's lived a cross old bachelor fer thirty year'
    and more—
A-lookin' glad and smilin'! And they's none o' you can
  say
That you can guess the reason why I feel so good to-day!

I must tell you all about it! But I'll have to deviate
A little in beginnin' so's to set the matter straight
As to how it comes to happen that I never took a wife—
Kind o' "crawfish" from the Present to the Spring-time
  of my life!

I was brought up in the country: Of a family of five—
Three brothers and a sister—I'm the only one alive,—
Fer they all died little babies; and 'twas one o' Mother's
  ways,
You know, to want a daughter; so she took a girl to raise.

The sweetest little thing she was, with rosy cheeks, and
  fat—

We was little chunks o' shavers then about as high as
    that!
But some way we sort o' *suited*-like! and Mother she'd
    declare
She never laid her eyes on a more lovin' pair

Than *we* was! So we growed up side by side fer thirteen
    year',
And every hour of it she growed to me more dear!—
W'y, even Father's dyin', as he did, I do believe
Warn't more affectin' to me than it was to see her grieve!

I was then a lad o' twenty; and I felt a flash o' pride
In thinkin' all depended on *me* now to pervide
Fer Mother and fer Mary; and I went about the place
With sleeves rolled up—and workin', with a mighty
    smilin' face.—

Fer *sompin' else* was workin'! but not a word I said
Of a certain sort o' notion that was runnin' through my
    head,—
"Some day I'd maybe marry, and a *brother's* love was one
Thing—a *lover's* was another!" was the way the notion
    run!

I remember onc't in harvest, when the "cradle-in" was
    done—
(When the harvest of my summers mounted up to
    twenty-one),

I was ridin' home with Mary at the closin' o' the day—
A-chawin' straws and thinkin', in a lover's lazy way!

And Mary's cheeks was burnin' like the sunset down the
 lane:
I noticed she was thinkin', too, and ast her to explain.
Well—when she turned and *kissed* me, *with her arms
 around me—law!*
I'd a bigger load o' Heaven than I had a load o' straw!

I don't p'tend to learnin', but I'll tell you what's a fac',
They's a mighty truthful sayin' somers in a almanac—
Er *somers*—'bout "puore happiness"—perhaps some
 folk'll laugh
At the idy—"only lastin' jest two seconds and a half."—

But it's jest as true as preachin'!—fer that was a *sister's*
 kiss,
And a sister's lovin' confidence a-tellin' to me this:—
"*She* was happy, *bein' promised to the son o' farmer
 Brown.*"—
And my feelin's struck a pardnership with sunset and
 went down!

I don't know *how* I acted, I don't know *what* I said,—
Fer my heart seemed jest a-turnin' to an ice-cold lump o'
 lead;

And the hosses kind o' glimmered before me in the road,
And the lines fell from my fingers—And that was all
    I knowed—

Fer—well, I don't know *how* long—They's a dim re-
    memberence
Of a sound o' snortin' hosses, and a stake-and-ridered
    fence
A-whizzin' past, and wheat-sheaves a-dancin' in the
    air,
And Mary screamin' "Murder!" and a-runnin' up to
    where

I was layin' by the roadside, and the wagon upside down
A-leanin' on the gate-post, with the wheels a-whirlin'
    round!
And I tried to raise and meet her, but I couldn't, with a
    vague
Sort o' notion comin' to me that I had a broken leg.

Well, the women nussed me through it; but many a
    time I'd sigh
As I'd keep a-gittin' better instid o' goin' to die,
And wonder what was left *me* worth livin' fer below,
When the girl I loved was married to another, don't you
    know!

And my thoughts was as rebellious as the folks was good
    and kind
When Brown and Mary married—Railly must 'a' been
    my *mind*
Was kind o' out o' kilter!—fer I hated Brown, you see,
Worse'n *pizen*—and the feller whittled crutches out fer
    me—

And done a thousand little ac's o' kindness and respec'—
And me a-wishin' all the time that I could break his
    neck!
My relief was like a mourner's when the funeral is done
When they moved to Illinois in the Fall o' Forty-one.

Then I went to work in airnest—I had nothin' much in
    view
But to drownd out rickollections—and it kep' me busy,
    too!
But I slowly thrived and prospered, tel Mother used to
    say
She expected yit to see me a wealthy man some day.

Then I'd think how little *money* was, compared to hap-
    piness—
And who'd be left to use it when I died I couldn't guess!
But I've still kep' speculatin' and a-gainin' year by year,
Tel I'm payin' half the taxes in the county, mighty near!

Well!—A year ago er better, a letter comes to hand
Astin' how I'd like to dicker fer some Illinois land—
"The feller that had owned it," it went ahead to state,
"Had jest deceased, insolvent, leavin' chance to specu-
    late,"—

And then it closed by sayin' that I'd "better come and
    see."—
I'd never been West, anyhow—a'most too wild fer *me*,
I'd allus had a notion; but a lawyer here in town
Said I'd find myself mistakend when I come to look
    around.

So I bids good-by to Mother, and I jumps aboard the
    train,
A-thinkin' what I'd bring her when I come back home
    again—
And ef she'd had an idy what the present was to be,
I think it's more'n likely she'd 'a' went along with me!

Cars is awful tejus ridin', fer all they go so fast!
But finally they called out my stoppin'-place at last:
And that night, at the tavern, I dreamp' I was a train
O' cars, and *skeered* at somepin', runnin' down a country
    lane!

Well, in the mornin' airly—after huntin' up the man—
The lawyer who was wantin' to swap the piece o' land—
We started fer the country; and I ast the history
Of the farm—its former owner—and so forth, etcetery!

And—well—it was inter*es*tin'—I su'prised him, I suppose
By the loud and frequent manner in which I blowed my nose!—
But his su'prise was greater, and it made him wonder more,
When I kissed and hugged the widder when she met us at the door!—

It was Mary: . . . They's a feelin' a-hidin' down in here—
Of course I can't explain it, ner ever make it clear.—
It was with us in that meetin', I don't want you to fergit!
And it makes me kind o' nervous when I think about it yit!

I *bought* that farm, and *deeded* it, afore I left the town,
With "title clear to mansions in the skies," to Mary Brown!
And fu'thermore, I took her and the *childern*—fer you see,
They'd never seed their Grandma—and I fetched 'em home with me.

So *now* you've got an idy why a man o' fifty-four,
Who's lived a cross old bachelor fer thirty year' and
    more,
Is a-lookin' glad and smilin'!—And I've jest come into
    town
To git a pair o' license fer to *marry* Mary Brown.

'MONGST THE HILLS O' SOMERSET

'MONGST the Hills o' Somerset
    Wisht I was a-roamin' yet!
    My feet won't get usen to
These low lands I'm trompin' through.
Wisht I could go back there, and
Stroke the long grass with my hand,
Kind o' like my sweetheart's hair
Smoothed out underneath it there!
Wisht I could set eyes once more
On our shadders, on before,
Climbin', in the airly dawn,
Up the slopes 'at love growed on
Natchurl as the violet
'Mongst the Hills o' Somerset!

How 't 'u'd rest a man like me
Jes' fer 'bout an hour to be
Up there where the morning air
Could reach out and ketch me there!—
Snatch my breath away, and then
Rensh and give it back again

Fresh as dew, and smellin' of
The old pinks I ust to love,
And a-flavor'n' ever' breeze
With mixt hints o' mulberries
And May-apples, from the thick
Bottom-lands along the crick
Where the fish bit, dry er wet,
'Mongst the Hills o' Somerset!

Like a livin' pictur' things
All comes back: the bluebird swings
In the maple, tongue and bill
Trillin' glory fit to kill!
In the orchard, jay and bee
Ripens the first pears fer me,
And the "Prince's Harvest" they
Tumble to me where I lay
In the clover, provin' still
"A boy's will is the wind's will."
Clean fergot is time, and care,
And thick hearin', and gray hair—
But they's nothin' I ferget
'Mongst the Hills o' Somerset!

Middle-aged—to be edzact,
Very middle-aged, in fact,—

Yet a-thinkin' back to then,
I'm the same wild boy again!
There's the dear old home once more,
And there's Mother at the door—
Dead, I know, fer thirty year',
Yet she's singin', and I hear;
And there's Jo, and Mary Jane,
And Pap, comin' up the lane!
Dusk's a-fallin'; and the dew,
'Pears like, it's a-fallin' too—
Dreamin' we're all livin' yet
'Mongst the Hills o' Somerset!

OLD JOHN HENRY

OLD John's jes' made o' the commonest stuff—
    Old John Henry—
  He's tough, I reckon,—but none too tough—
Too tough though's better than not enough!
    Says old John Henry.
He does his best, and when his best's bad,
He don't fret none, ner he don't git sad—
He simply 'lows it's the best he had:
    Old John Henry!

His doctern's jes' o' the plainest brand—
    Old John Henry—
A smilin' face and a hearty hand
'S religen 'at all folks understand,
    Says old John Henry.
He's stove up some with the rhumatiz,
And they hain't no shine on them shoes o' his,
And his hair hain't cut—but his eye-teeth is:
    Old John Henry!

He feeds hisse'f when the stock's all fed—
> Old John Henry—

And sleeps like a babe when he goes to bed—
And dreams o' Heaven and home-made bread,
> Says old John Henry.

He hain't refined as he'd ort to be
To fit the statutes o' poetry,
Ner his clothes don't fit him—but *he* fits *me:*
> Old John Henry!

"HOME AG'IN"

I'M a-feelin' ruther sad,
    Fer a father proud and glad
    As *I* am—my only child
Home, and all so rickonciled!
Feel so strange-like, and don't know
What the mischief ails me so!
'Stid o' bad, I ort to be
Feelin' good pertickerly—
Yes, and extry thankful, too,
'Cause my nearest kith and kin,
My Elviry's schoolin' 's through,
And I' got her home ag'in—
        Home ag'in with me!

Same as ef her mother'd been
Livin', I have done my best
By the girl, and watchfulest;
Nussed her—keerful' as I could—
From a baby, day and night,—
Drawin' on the neighberhood
And the women-folks as light

As needsessity 'ud 'low—
'Cept in "teethin'," onc't, and fight
Through black-measles. Don't know now
How we ever saved the child!
Doc *he'd* give her up, and said,
As I stood there by the bed
Sort o' foolin' with her hair
On the hot, wet pillar there,
"Wuz no use!"—And at them-air
Very words she waked and smiled—
Yes, and *knowed* me. And that's where
I broke down, and simply jes'
Bellered like a boy—I guess!—
Women claim I did, but I
Allus helt I didn't cry
But wuz laughin',—and I *wuz*,—
Men don't cry like *women* does!
Well, right then and there I felt
'T 'uz her mother's doin's, and,
Jes' like to mys'f, I knelt
Whisperin', "I understand." . . .
So I've raised her, you might say,
Stric'ly in the narrer way
'At her mother walked therein—
Not so quite religiously,

Yit still strivin'-like to do
Ever'thing a father *could*
Do he knowed the *mother* would
Ef she'd lived—And now all's through
And I' got her home ag'in—
    Home ag'in with me!

And I' been so lonesome, too,
Here o' late, especially,—
"Old Aunt Abigail," you know,
Ain't no company;—and so
Jes' the hired hand, you see—
Jonas—like a relative
More—sence he come here to live
With us, nigh ten year' ago.
Still he don't count much, you know,
In the way o' company—
Lonesome, 'peared-like, 'most as me!
So, as *I* say, I' been so
Special lonesome-like and blue,
With Elviry, like she's been,
'Way so much, last two or three
Year'—But now she's home ag'in—
    Home ag'in with me!
Driv in fer her yisterday,
Me and Jonas—gay and spry,—
We jes' cut up, all the way!—

Yes, and sung!—tel, blame it! I
Keyed my voice up 'bout as high
As when—days 'at I wuz young—
"Buckwheat-notes" wuz all they sung.
Jonas bantered me, and 'greed
To sing one 'at town-folks sing
Down at Split Stump 'er High-Low—
Some new "ballet," said he, 'at he'd
Learnt—about "The Grape-vine Swing."
And when *he* quit, *I* begun
To chune up my voice and run
Through the what's-called "scales" and "do
Sol-me-fa's" I *ust* to know—
Then let loose old favor*ite* one,
"Hunters o' Kentucky!" *My!*
Tel I thought the boy would *die!*
And we *both* laughed—Yes, and still
Heerd more laughin', top the hill;
Fer we'd missed Elviry's train,
And she'd lit out 'crost the fields,—
Dewdrops dancin' at her heels,
And cut up old Smoots's lane
So's to meet us. And there in
Shadder o' the chinkypin,
With a danglin' dogwood-bough
Bloomin' 'bove her—See her now!—
Sunshine sort o' flickerin' down

And a kind o' laughin' all
Round her new red parasol,
Tryin' to git at *her!*—well—like
I jumped out and showed 'em how—
Yes, and jes' the place to strike
That-air mouth o' hern—as sweet
As the blossoms breshed her brow
Er sweet-williams round her feet—
White and blushy, too, as she
"Howdied" up to Jonas, and
Jieuked her head, and waved her hand
"Hey!" says I, as she bounced in
The spring-wagon, reachin' back
To give *me* a lift, "whoop-ee!"
I-says-ee, "you're home ag'in—
    Home ag'in with me!"

Lord! how *wild* she wuz, and glad,
Gittin' home!—and things she had
To inquire about, and talk—
Plowin', plantin', and the stock—
News o' neighborhood; and how
Wuz the Deem-girls doin' now,
Sence that-air young chicken-hawk
They was "tamin'" soared away
With their settin'-hen, one day?—

(Said she'd got Mame's postal-card
'Bout it, very day 'at she
Started home from Bethany.)
How wuz produce—eggs, and lard?—
Er wuz stores still claimin' "hard
Times," as usual? And, says she,
Troubled-like, "How's Deedie—say?
Sence pore child e-loped away
And got back, and goin' to 'ply
Fer school-license by and by—
And where's 'Lijy workin' at?
And how's 'Aunt' and 'Uncle Jake'?
How wuz 'Old Maje'—and the cat?
And wuz Marthy's baby fat
As his 'Humpty-Dumpty' ma?
Sweetest thing she ever saw!—
Must run 'crost and see her, too,
Soon as she turned in and got
Supper fer us—smokin'-hot—
And the 'dishes' all wuz through.—"
Sich a supper! W'y, I set
There and et, and et, and et!—
Jes' et on, tel Jonas he
Pushed his chair back, laughed, and says,
"I could walk *his* log!" and we
All laughed then, tel 'Viry she

Lit the lamp—and I give in!—
Riz and kissed her: "Heaven bless
You!" says I—"you're home ag'in—
Same old dimple in your chin,
Same white apern," I-says-ee,
"Same sweet girl, and good to see
As your *mother* ust to be,—
And I' got you home ag'in—
    Home ag'in with me!"

I turns then to go on by her
Through the door—and see her eyes
Both wuz swimmin', and she tries
To say somepin'—can't—and so
Grabs and hugs and lets me go.
Noticed Aunty'd made a fire
In the settin'-room and gone
Back where her p'serves wuz on
Bilin' in the kitchen. I
Went out on the porch and set,
Thinkin'-like. And by and by
Heerd Elviry, soft and low,
At the organ, kind o' go
A mi-anderin' up and down
With her fingers 'mongst the keys—
"Vacant Chair" and "Old Camp-Groun'."

Dusk was moist-like, with a breeze
Lazin' round the locus'-trees—
Heerd the hosses champin', and
Jonas feedin', and the hogs—
Yes, and katydids and frogs—
And a tree-toad, somers. Heerd
Also whipperwills.—*My land!*—
All so mournful ever'where—
Them out here, and her in there,—
'Most like 'tendin' *services!*
Anyway, I must 'a' jes
Kind o' drapped asleep, I guess;
'Cause when Jonas must 'a' passed
Me, a-comin' in, I knowed
Nothin' of it—yit it seemed
Sort o' like I kind o' dreamed
'Bout him, too, a-slippin' in,
And a-watchin' back to see
Ef I *wuz* asleep, and then
Passin' in where 'Viry wuz;
And where I declare it does
'Pear to me I heerd him say,
Wild and glad and whisperin'—
'Peared-like heerd him say, says-ee,
"Ah! I got you home ag'in—
     Home ag'in with me!"

CASSANDER

"CASSANDER! *O* Cassander!"—her *mother's
voice* seems cle'r
    As ever, from the old back-porch, a-hollerin'
fer her—
Specially in airly Spring—like May, two year' ago—
Last time she hollered fer her,—and Cassander didn't
hear!

Cassander wuz so chirpy-like and sociable and free,
And good to ever'body, and wuz even good to me
    Though *I* wuz jes' a common—well, a farm-hand,
don't you know,
A-workin' on her father's place, as pore as pore could be!

Her bein' jes' a' only child, Cassander had her way
A good-'eal more'n other girls; and neighbers ust to say
    She looked most like her Mother, but wuz turned most
like her Pap,—
Except *he* had no use fer *town*-folks then—ner *yit to-
day!*

I can't claim she incouraged *me:* She'd let me drive her in
To town sometimes, on Saturd'ys, and fetch her home ag'in,
   Tel onc't she 'scused "Old Moll" and me,—and some blame' city-chap,
He driv her home, two-forty style, in face o' kith and kin.

She even tried to make him stay fer supper, but I 'low
He must 'a' kind o' 'spicioned some objections.—Anyhow,
   Her mother callin' at her, whilse her father stood and shook
His fist,—the town-chap turnt his team and made his partin' bow.

"Cassander! *You*, Cassander!"—hear her mother jes' as plain,
And see Cassander blushin' like the peach-tree down the lane,
   Whilse I sneaked on apast her, with a sort o' hang-dog look,
A-feelin' cheap as sorghum and as green as sugar-cane!

(You see, I'd *skooted* when she met her *town*-beau—
    when, in fact,
Ef I'd had sense I'd *stayed* fer her.—But sense wuz what
    I lacked!
  So I'd cut home ahead o' her, so's I could tell 'em what
Wuz keepin' her. And—*you* know how a jealous fool'll
    act!)

I past her, I wuz sayin',—but she never turnt her head;
I swallered-like and cle'red my th'oat—but that wuz all
    I said;
  And whilse I hoped fer some word back, it wuzn't
    what I got.—
That girl'll not stay stiller on the day she's layin' dead!

Well, that-air silence *lasted!*—Ust to listen ever' day
I'd be at work and hear her mother callin' thataway;
  I'd *sight* Cassander, mayby, cuttin' home acrost the
    blue
And drizzly fields; but nary answer—nary word to say!

Putt in about two weeks o' that—two weeks o' rain and
    mud,
Er mostly so: I couldn't plow. The old crick like a
    flood:

And, lonesome as a borried dog, I'd wade them old woods through—
The dogwood blossoms white as snow, and redbuds red as blood.

Last time her mother called her—sich a morning like as now:
The robins and the bluebirds, and the blossoms on the bough—
   And this wuz yit 'fore brekfust, with the sun out at his best,
And hosses kickin' in the barn—and dry enough to plow.

"Cassander! *O* Cassander!" ... And her only answer— What?—
A letter, twisted round the cookstove damper, smokin'-hot,
   A-statin': "I wuz married on that day of all the rest,
The day my husband fetched me home—ef you ain't all fergot!"

"Cassander! *O* Cassander!" seems, allus, 'long in May,
I hear her mother callin' her—a-callin', night and day—
   "Cassander! *O* Cassander!" allus callin', as I say,
"Cassander! *O* Cassander!" jes a-callin' thataway.

WE MUST GET HOME

WE MUST get home! How could we stray
    like this?—
    So far from home, we know not where it
is,—
Only in some fair, apple-blossomy place
Of children's faces—and the mother's face—
We dimly dream it, till the vision clears
Even in the eyes of fancy, glad with tears.

We must get home—for we have been away
So long, it seems forever and a day!
And O so very homesick we have grown,
The laughter of the world is like a moan
In our tired hearing, and its songs as vain,—
We must get home—we must get home again!

We must get home! With heart and soul we yearn
To find the long-lost pathway, and return! ...
The child's shout lifted from the questing band
Of old folk, faring weary, hand in hand,

But faces brightening, as if clouds at last
Were showering sunshine on us as they passed.

We must get home: It hurts so, staying here,
Where fond hearts must be wept out tear by tear,
And where to wear wet lashes means, at best,
When most our lack, the least our hope of rest—
When most our need of joy, the more our pain—
We must get home—we must get home again!

We must get home—home to the simple things—
The morning-glories twirling up the strings
And bugling color, as they blared in blue-
And-white o'er garden-gates we scampered through;
The long grape-arbor, with its under-shade
Blue as the green and purple overlaid.

We must get home: All is so quiet there:
The touch of loving hands on brow and hair—
Dim rooms, wherein the sunshine is made mild—
The lost love of the mother and the child
Restored in restful lullabies of rain,—
We must get home—we must get home again!

The rows of sweetcorn and the China beans
Beyond the lettuce-beds where, towering, leans

The giant sunflower in barbaric pride
Guarding the barn-door and the lane outside;
The honeysuckles, midst the hollyhocks,
That clamber almost to the martin-box.

We must get home, where, as we nod and drowse,
Time humors us and tiptoes through the house,
And loves us best when sleeping baby-wise,
With dreams—not tear-drops—brimming our clenched
    eyes,—
Pure dreams that know nor taint nor earthly stain—
We must get home—we must get home again!

We must get home! There only may we find
The little playmates that we left behind,—
Some racing down the road; some by the brook;
Some droning at their desks, with wistful look
Across the fields and orchards—farther still
Where laughs and weeps the old wheel at the mill.

We must get home! The willow-whistle's call
Trills crisp and liquid as the waterfall—
Mocking the trillers in the cherry-trees
And making discord of such rhymes as these,
That know nor lilt nor cadence but the birds
First warbled—then all poets afterwards.

We must get home; and, unremembering there
All gain of all ambition otherwhere,
Rest—from the feverish victory, and the crown
Of conquest whose waste glory weighs us down.—
Fame's fairest gifts we toss back with disdain—
We must get home—we must get home again!

We must get home again—we must—we must!—
(Our rainy faces pelted in the dust)
Creep back from the vain quest through endless strife
To find not anywhere in all of life
A happier happiness than blest us then. . . .
We must get home—we must get home again!

US FARMERS IN THE COUNTRY

US FARMERS in the country, as the seasons go
    and come,
  Is purty much like other folks,—we're apt to
    grumble some!
The Spring's too back'ard fer us, er too for'ard—ary
    one—
We'll jaw about it anyhow, and have our way er none!

The thaw's set in too suddent; er the frost's stayed in the
    soil
Too long to give the wheat a chance, and crops is bound
    to spoil.
The weather's eether most too mild, er too outrageous
    rough,
And altogether too much rain, er not half rain enugh!

Now what I'd like and what you'd like is plane enugh to
    see:
It's jest to have old Providence drop round on you and me
And ast us what our views is first, regardin' shine er rain,
And post 'em when to shet her off, er let her on again!

And yit I'd ruther, after all—consider'n' other chores
I' got on hands, a-tendin' both to my affares and yours—
I'd ruther miss the blame I'd git, a-rulin' things up thare,
And spend my extry time in praise and gratitude and
    prayer.

A CHILD'S HOME—LONG AGO

EVEN as the gas-flames flicker to and fro,
    The Old Man's wavering fancies leap and glow—
As o'er the vision, like a mirage, falls
The old log cabin with its dingy walls,
And crippled chimney with its crutch-like prop
Beneath a sagging shoulder at the top:
The coonskin battened fast on either side—
The wisps of leaf-tobacco—"cut-and-dried";
The yellow strands of quartered apples, hung
In rich festoons that tangle in among
The morning-glory vines that clamber o'er
The little clapboard roof above the door:
The old well-sweep that drops a courtesy
To every thirsting soul so graciously,
The stranger, as he drains the dripping gourd,
Intuitively murmurs, "Thank the Lord!"
Again through mists of memory arise
The simple scenes of home before the eyes:—
The happy mother, humming, with her wheel,
The dear old melodies that used to steal

So drowsily upon the summer air,
The house-dog hid his bone, forgot his care,
And nestled at her feet, to dream, perchance,
Some cooling dream of winter-time romance:
The square of sunshine through the open door
That notched its edge across the puncheon floor,
And made a golden coverlet whereon
The god of slumber had a picture drawn
Of Babyhood, in all the loveliness
Of dimpled cheek and limb and linsey dress:
The bough-filled fireplace, and the mantel wide,
Its fire-scorched ankles stretched on either side,
Where, perched upon its shoulders 'neath the joist,
The old clock hiccoughed, harsh and husky-voiced,
And snarled the premonition, dire and dread,
When it should hammer Time upon the head:
Tomatoes, red and yellow, in a row,
Preserved not then for diet, but for show,—
Like rare and precious jewels in the rough
Whose worth was not appraised at half enough:
The jars of jelly, with their dusty tops;
The bunch of pennyroyal; the cordial drops;
The flask of camphor, and the vial of squills,
The box of buttons, garden-seeds, and pills;
And, ending all the mantel's bric-à-brac,
The old, time-honored "Family Almanack."

And memory, with a mother's touch of love,
Climbs with us to the dusky loft above,
Where drowsily we trail our fingers in
The mealy treasures of the harvest bin;
And, feeling with our hands the open track,
We pat the bag of barley on the back;
And, groping onward through the mellow gloom,
We catch the hidden apple's faint perfume,
And, mingling with it, fragrant hints of pear
And musky melon ripening somewhere.
Again we stretch our limbs upon the bed
Where first our simple childish prayers were said;
And while, without, the gallant cricket trills
A challenge to the solemn whippoorwills,
And, filing on the chorus with his glee,
The katydid whets all the harmony
To feather-edge of incoherent song,
We drop asleep, and peacefully along
The current of our dreams we glide away
To the dim harbor of another day.

A VOICE FROM THE FARM

IT IS my dream to have you here with me,
   Out of the heated city's dust and din—
   Here where the colts have room to gambol in,
And kine to graze, in clover to the knee.
I want to see your wan face happily
   Lit with the wholesome smiles that have not been
   In use since the old games you used to win
When we pitched horseshoes: And I want to be
   At utter loaf with you in this dim land
     Of grove and meadow, while the crickets make
       Our own talk tedious, and the bat wields
His bulky flight, as we cease converse and
     In a dusk like velvet smoothly take
       Our way toward home across the dewy fields.

HOME-FOLKS

HOME-FOLKS!—Well, that-air name, to me
  Sounds jis the same as *poetry*—
  That is, ef poetry is jis
As sweet as I've hearn tell it is!

Home-Folks—they're jis the same as *kin*—
All brung up, same as *we* have bin,
Without no overpowerin' sense
Of their oncommon consequence!

They've bin to school, but not to git
The habit fastened on 'em yit
So as to ever interfere
With *other* work 'at's waitin' here:

Home-Folks has crops to plant and plow,
Er lives in town and keeps a cow;
But whether country-jakes er town-,
They know when eggs is up er down!

La! can't you *spot* 'em—when you meet
'Em *anywheres*—in field er street?
And can't you see their faces, bright
As circus-day, heave into sight?

And can't you hear their "Howdy!" clear
As a brook's chuckle to the ear,
And allus find their laughin' eyes
As fresh and clear as morning skies?

And can't you—when they've gone away
Jis feel 'em shakin' hands, all day?
And feel, too, you've bin higher raised
By sich a meetin'?—God be praised!

Oh, Home-Folks! you're the best of all
'At ranges this terreschul ball,—
But, north er south, er east er west,
It's home is where you're at your best.—

It's home—it's home your faces shine,
In-nunder your own fig and vine—
Your fambly and your neighbers 'bout
Ye, and the latch-string hangin' out

. . . .

Home-Folks—*at home*,—I know o' one
Old feller now 'at hain't got none.—
Invite him—he may hold back some—
But *you* invite him, and he'll come.

THE HOOSIER FOLK-CHILD

THE Hoosier Folk-Child—all unsung—
  Unlettered all of mind and tongue;
  Unmastered, unmolested—made
Most wholly frank and unafraid:
Untaught of any school—unvexed
Of law or creed—all unperplexed—
Unsermoned, ay, and undefiled,
An all imperfect-perfect child—
A type which (Heaven forgive us!) you
And I do tardy honor to,
And so profane the sanctities
Of our most sacred memories.
Who, growing thus from boy to man,
That dares not be American?
Go, Pride, with prudent underbuzz—
Go *whistle!* as the Folk-Child does.

The Hoosier Folk-Child's world is not
Much wider than the stable-lot
Between the house and highway fence
That bounds the home his father rents.

His playmates mostly are the ducks
And chickens, and the boy that "shucks
Corn by the shock," and talks of town,
And whether eggs are "up" or "down,"
And prophesies in boastful tone
Of "owning horses of his own,"
And "being his own man," and "when
He gets to be, what he'll do then."—
Takes out his jack-knife dreamily
And makes the Folk-Child two or three
Crude corn-stalk figures,—a wee span
Of horses and a little man.

The Hoosier Folk-Child's eyes are wise
And wide and round as Brownies' eyes:
The smile they wear is ever blent
With all-expectant wonderment,—
On homeliest things they bend a look
As rapt as o'er a picture-book,
And seem to ask, whate'er befall,
The happy reason of it all:—
Why grass is all so glad a green,
And leaves—and what their lispings mean;—
Why buds grow on the boughs, and why
They burst in blossom by and by—
As though the orchard in the breeze
Had shook and popped its *pop-corn trees*,

To lure and whet, as well they might,
Some seven-league giant's appetite!

The Hoosier Folk-Child's chubby face
Has scant refinement, caste or grace,—
From crown to chin, and cheek to cheek,
It bears the grimy water-streak
Of rinsings such as some long rain
Might drool across the window-pane
Wherethrough he peers, with troubled frown,
As some lorn team drives by for town.
His brow is elfed with wispish hair,
With tangles in it here and there,
As though the warlocks snarled it so
At midmirk when the moon sagged low,
And boughs did toss and skreek and shake,
And children moaned themselves awake,
With fingers clutched, and starting sight
Blind as the blackness of the night!

The Hoosier Folk-Child!—Rich is he
In all the wealth of poverty!
He owns nor title nor estate,
Nor speech but half articulate,—
He owns nor princely robe nor crown;—
Yet, draped in patched and faded brown,
He owns the bird-songs of the hills—
The laughter of the April rills;

And his are all the diamonds set
In Morning's dewy coronet,—
And his the Dusk's first minted stars
That twinkle through the pasture-bars
And litter all the skies at night
With glittering scraps of silver light;—
The rainbow's bar, from rim to rim,
In beaten gold, belongs to him.

WHAT SMITH KNEW ABOUT FARMING

THERE wasn't two purtier farms in the state
   Than the couple of which I'm about to relate;—
   Jinin' each other—belongin' to Brown,
And jest at the edge of a flourishin' town.
Brown was a man, as I understand,
That allus had handled a good 'eal o' land,
And was sharp as a tack in drivin' a trade—
For that's the way most of his money was made.
And all the grounds and the orchards about
His two pet farms was all tricked out
With poppies and posies
And sweet-smellin' rosies;
And hundreds o' kinds
Of all sorts o' vines,
To tickle the most horticultural minds;
And little dwarf trees not as thick as your wrist
With ripe apples on 'em as big as your fist:
And peaches,—Siberian crabs and pears,
And quinces—Well! *any* fruit *any* tree bears;
And the purtiest stream—jest a-swimmin' with fish,
And—*jest a'most everything heart could wish!*

The purtiest orch'rds—I wish you could see
How purty they was, fer I know it 'ud be
A regular treat!—but I'll go ahead with
My story! A man by the name o' Smith—
(A bad name to rhyme,
But I reckon that I'm
Not goin' back on a Smith! nary time!)
'At hadn't a soul of kin nor kith,
And more money than he knowed what to do with,—
So he comes a-ridin' along one day,
And *he* says to Brown, in his offhand way—
Who was trainin' some newfangled vines round a bay-
Winder—"Howdy-do—look-a-here—say:
What'll you take fer this property here?—
I'm talkin' o' leavin' the city this year,
And I want to be
Where the air is free,
And I'll *buy* this place, if it ain't too dear!"—
Well—they grumbled and jawed aroun'—
"I don't like to part with the place," says Brown;
"Well," says Smith, a-jerkin' his head,
"That house yonder—bricks painted red—
Jest like this'n—a *purtier view*—
Who is it owns *it?*" "That's mine too,"
Says Brown, as he winked at a hole in his shoe,
"But I'll tell you right here jest what I *kin* do:—
If you'll pay the figgers I'll sell *it* to you."

Smith went over and looked at the place—
Badgered with Brown, and argied the case—
Thought that Brown's figgers was rather too tall,
But, findin' that Brown wasn't goin' to fall,
In final agreed,
So they drawed up the deed
Fer the farm and the fixtures—the live stock an' all
And so Smith moved from the city as soon
As he possibly could—But "the man in the moon"
Knowed more'n Smith o' farmin' pursuits,
And jest to convince you, and have no disputes,
How little he knowed,
I'll tell you his "mode,"
As he called it, o' raisin' "the best that growed,"
In the way o' potatoes—
Cucumbers—tomatoes,
And squashes as lengthy as young alligators.
'Twas allus a curious thing to me
How big a fool a feller kin be
When he gits on a farm after leavin' a town!—
Expectin' to raise himself up to renown,
And reap fer himself agricultural fame,
By growin' of squashes—*without any shame*—
As useless and long as a technical name.
To make the soil pure,
And certainly sure,
He plastered the ground with patent manure.

He had cultivators, and double-hoss plows,
And patent machines fer milkin' his cows;
And patent hay-forks—patent measures and weights,
And new patent back-action hinges fer gates,
And barn locks and latches, and such little dribs
And patents to keep the rats out o' the cribs—
Reapers and mowers,
And patent grain sowers;
And drillers
And tillers
And cucumber hillers,
And harriers;—and had patent rollers and scrapers,
And took about ten agricultural papers.
So you can imagine how matters turned out:
But *Brown* didn't have not a shadder o' doubt
That Smith didn't know what he was about
When he said that "the *old* way to farm was played out."
But Smith worked ahead,
And when any one said
That the *old* way o' workin' was better instead
O' his "modern idees," he allus turned red,
And wanted to know
What made people so
Infernally anxious to hear theirselves crow?
And guessed that he'd manage to hoe his own row.
Brown he come onc't and leant over the fence,
And told Smith that he couldn't see any sense

In goin' to such a tremendous expense
Fer the sake o' such no-account expeeriments:—
"That'll never make corn!
As shore's you're born
It'll come out the leetlest end of the horn!"
Says Brown, as he pulled off a big roastin'-ear
From a stalk of his own
That had tribble outgrown
Smith's poor yaller shoots, and says he, "Looky here!
This corn was raised in the old-fashioned way,
And I rather imagine that *this* corn'll pay
Expenses fer *raisin'* it!—What do you say?"
Brown got him then to look over his crop.—
His luck that season had been tip-top!
And you may surmise
Smith opened his eyes
And let out a look o' the wildest surprise
When Brown showed him punkins as big as the lies
He was stuffin' him with—about offers he's had
Fer his farm: "I don't want to sell very bad,"
He says, but says he,
"Mr. Smith, you kin see
Fer yourself how matters is standin' with me,
I understand farmin' and I'd better stay,
You know, on my farm;—I'm a-makin' it pay—

I oughtn't to grumble!—I reckon I'll clear
Away over four thousand dollars this year."
And that was the reason, he made it appear,
Why he didn't care about sellin' his farm,
And hinted at his havin' done himself harm
In sellin' the other, and wanted to know
If Smith wouldn't sell back ag'in to him.—So
Smith took the bait, and says he, "Mr. Brown,
I wouldn't *sell* out, but we might swap aroun'—
How'll you trade your place fer mine?"
(Purty sharp way o' comin' the shine
Over Smith! Wasn't it?) Well, sir, this Brown
Played out his hand and brought Smithy down—
Traded with him an', workin' it cute,
Raked in two thousand dollars to boot
As slick as a whistle, an' that wasn't all,—
He managed to trade back ag'in the next fall,
And the next—and the next—as long as Smith stayed
He reaped with his harvests an annual trade.—
Why, I reckon that Brown must 'a' easily made—
On an *average*—nearly two thousand a year—
Together he made over seven thousand—clear.—
Till Mr. Smith found he was losin' his health
In as big a proportion, almost, as his wealth;

So at last he concluded to move back to town,
And sold back his farm to this same Mr. Brown
At very low figgers, by gittin' it down.
Further'n this I have nothin' to say
Than merely advisin' the Smiths fer to stay
In their grocery stores in flourishin' towns
And leave agriculture alone—and the Browns.

HOME AT NIGHT

WHEN chirping crickets fainter cry,
And pale stars blossom in the sky,
And twilight's gloom has dimmed the bloom
And blurred the butterfly:

When locust-blossoms fleck the walk,
And up the tiger-lily stalk
The glow-worm crawls and clings and falls
And glimmers down the garden-walls:

When buzzing things, with double wings
Of crisp and raspish flutterings,
Go whizzing by so very nigh
One thinks of fangs and stings:—

O then, within, is stilled the din
Of crib she rocks the baby in,
And heart and gate and latch's weight
Are lifted—and the lips of Kate.

A CANARY AT THE FARM

FOLKS has be'n to town, and Sahry
Fetched 'er home a pet canary,—
And of all the blame', contrary,
   Aggervatin' things alive!
I love music—that's I love it
When it's *free*—and plenty of it;—
But I kindo' git above it,
   At a dollar-eighty-five!

Reason's plain as I'm a-sayin'—
Jes' the idy, now, o' layin'
Out yer money, and a-payin'
   Fer a willer-cage and bird,
When the medder-larks is wingin'
Round you, and the woods is ringin'
With the beautifullest singin'
   That a mortal ever heard!

Sahry's sot, tho'.—So I tell her
He's a purty little feller,
With his wings o' creamy-yeller,
   And his eyes keen as a cat;
And the twitter o' the critter
'Pears to absolutely glitter!
Guess I'll haf to go and git her
   A high-priceter cage 'n that!

HOOSIER SPRING-POETRY

WHEN ever'thing's a-goin' like she's got-a-
    goin' now,—
  The maple-sap a-drippin', and the buds on
ever' bough
A-sort o' reachin' up'ards all a-trimblin', ever' one,
Like 'bout a million brownie-fists a-shakin' at the sun!
The childern wants their shoes off 'fore their breakfast,
    and the Spring
Is here so good-and-plenty that the old hen has to sing!—
When things is goin' *thisaway*, w'y, that's the sign, you
    know,
That ever'thing's a-goin' like we like to see her go!

Oh, ever'thing's a-goin' like we like to see her go!
Old Winter's up and dusted, with his dratted frost and
    snow—
The ice is out the crick ag'in, the freeze is out the ground,
And you'll see faces thawin' too ef you'll jes' look
    around!—

The bluebird's landin' home ag'in, and glad to git the chance,
'Cause here's where he belongs at, that's a settled circumstance!
And him and mister robin now's a-chunin' fer the show.
Oh, ever'thing's a-goin' like we like to see her go!

The sun ain't jes' p'tendin' *now!*—The ba'm is in the breeze—
The trees'll soon be green as grass, and grass as green as trees;
The buds is all jes' *eechin'*, and the dogwood down the run
Is bound to bu'st out laughin' 'fore another week is done;
The bees is wakin', gap'y-like, and fumblin' fer their buzz,
A-thinkin', ever-wakefuler, of other days that wuz,—
When all the land wuz orchard-blooms and clover, don't you know. . . .
Oh, ever'thing's a-goin' like we like to see her go!

ON THE BANKS O' DEER CRICK

ON THE banks o' Deer Crick! There's the place
    fer me!—
Worter slidin' past ye jes' as clair as it kin be:
See yer shadder in it, and the shadder o' the sky,
And the shadder o' the buzzard as he goes a-lazin' by;
Shadder o' the pizen-vines, and shadder o' the trees—
And I purt' nigh said the shadder o' the sunshine and the
    breeze!
Well—I never seen the ocean ner I never seen the sea:
On the banks o' Deer Crick's grand enough fer me!

On the banks o' Deer Crick—mil'd er two from town—
'Long up where the mill-race comes a-loafin' down,—
Like to git up in there—'mongst the sycamores—
And watch the worter at the dam, a-frothin' as she pours;
Crawl out on some old log, with my hook and line,
Where the fish is jes' so thick you kin see 'em shine
As they flicker round yer bait, *coaxin'* you to jerk,
Tel yer tired ketchin' of 'em, mighty nigh, as *work!*

On the banks o' Deer Crick!—Allus my delight
Jes' to be around there—take it day er night!—
Watch the snipes and killdees foolin' half the day
Er these-'ere little worter-bugs skootin' ever' way!—
Snake-feeders glancin' round, er dartin' out o' sight;
And dewfall, and bullfrogs, and lightnin'-bugs at night—
Stars up through the tree-tops—er in the crick below,—
And smell o' mussrat through the dark clean from the old by-o!

Er take a tromp, some Sund'y, say, 'way up to "Johnson's Hole,"
And find where he's had a fire, and hid his fishin'-pole:
Have yer "dog-leg" with ye, and yer pipe and "cut-and-dry"—
Pocketful o' corn-bread, and slug er two o' rye,—
Soak yer hide in sunshine and waller in the shade—
Like the Good Book tells us—"where there're none to make afraid!"
Well!—I never seen the ocean ner I never seen the sea—
On the banks o' Deer Crick's grand enough fer me!

OLD MAN'S NURSERY RHYME

IN the jolly winters
   Of the long-ago,
     It was not so cold as now—
Oh! No! No!
Then, as I remember,
   Snowballs to eat
Were as good as apples now,
   And every bit as sweet!

In the jolly winters
   Of the dead-and-gone,
Bub was warm as summer,
   With his red mitts on,—
Just in his little waist-
   And-pants all together,
Who ever heard him growl
   About cold weather?

In the jolly winters
   Of the long-ago—
Was it *half* so cold as now?
   Oh! No! No!
Who caught his death o' cold,
   Making prints of men
Flat-backed in snow that now's
   Twice as cold again?

In the jolly winters
   Of the dead-and-gone,
Startin' out rabbit huntin'—
   Early as the dawn,—
Who ever froze his fingers,
   Ears, heels, or toes,—
Or'd 'a' cared if he had?
   Nobody knows!

Nights by the kitchen stove,
   Shellin' white and red
Corn in the skillet, and
   Sleepin' four abed!
Ah! the jolly winters
   Of the long-ago!
We were not as old as now—
   Oh! No! No!

THE MULBERRY TREE

O, IT'S many's the scenes which is dear to my mind
As I think of my childhood so long left behind;
The home of my birth, with its old puncheon-floor,
And the bright morning-glorys that growed round the door;
The warped clabboard roof whare the rain it run off
Into streams of sweet dreams as I laid in the loft,
Countin' all of the joys that was dearest to me,
And a-thinkin' the most of the mulberry tree.

And to-day as I dream, with both eyes wide-awake,
I can see the old tree, and its limbs as they shake,
And the long purple berries that rained on the ground
Whare the pastur' was bald whare we trommpt it around.
And again, peekin' up through the thick leafy shade,
I can see the glad smiles of the friends when I strayed
With my little bare feet from my own mother's knee
To foller them off to the mulberry tree.

Leanin' up in the forks, I can see the old rail,
And the boy climbin' up it, claw, tooth, and toe-nail,
And in fancy can hear, as he spits on his hands,
The ring of his laugh and the rip of his pants.
But that rail led to glory, as certin and shore
As I'll never climb thare by that rout' any more—
What was all the green lauruls of Fame unto me,
With my brows in the boughs of the mulberry tree!

Then it's who can fergit the old mulberry tree
That he knowed in the days when his thoughts was as
    free
As the flutterin' wings of the birds that flew out
Of the tall wavin' tops as the boys come about?
O, a crowd of my memories, laughin' and gay,
Is a-climbin' the fence of that pastur' to-day,
And a-pantin' with joy, as us boys ust to be,
They go racin' acrost fer the mulberry tree.

www.ingramcontent.com/pod-product-compliance
Lightning Source LLC
Chambersburg PA
CBHW010855090426
42737CB00019B/3377